"Eryn has committed her life to helping others know their value. Here, we get to pull back the curtain and discover the hurt behind this hopeful healer. Each page is packed with warmth, wisdom, and heartfelt honesty. This soul-affirming book is much like the heart of its author—effervescent and expansive."

Brad Montague, *New York Times* bestselling author, illustrator, and creator of Kid President

"Eryn Eddy is a dreamer. And for those of us with hopes and dreams (and that includes you), life can be hard on us. That's why *So Worth Loving* is an important book. Eryn shares her story with authenticity, candor, and hope, reminding you that the dreams in you are worth pursuing because you are so worth loving."

Jeff Henderson, author of *Know What You're FOR: A Growth Strategy for Work, An Even Better Strategy for Life*

"Reading *So Worth Loving* is like taking a plunge off a cliff into a clear waterfall of honesty, healing, and hope. Eryn Eddy grabs you by the hand, leans her head in, and, with a joyous twinkle, dares you to jump—with her going first. When you rise to the surface, you'll gulp the fresh air of discovery. There you are! And there is the one true God who knows you through and through, loves you just the way you are, and assures you that there's nothing you can do about it. Indeed, you *are* so worth loving!"

Elisa Morgan, speaker; author, *When We Pray Like Jesus*; cohost, *Discover the Word*; president emerita, MOPS International

"'*I needed this.*' Comb through the responses to the stories Eryn and So Worth Loving have shared online in the past decade and these are the words you'll find over and over again. My reaction to Eryn's formal diary, *So Worth Loving*, is no different. I needed this book. You might too."

Mary Chau, lettering artist, maker of things, and proud friend of Eryn Eddy

"Not only is this book good, it caused me to change the story I tell myself. Everyone needs this book."

Jeff Shinabarger, founder of Plywood People
and coauthor of *Love or Work*

"Eryn's voice is just what our world needs right now. She writes so beautifully of owning your story, becoming accountable for your own life, and empowering yourself through your faith. In a world inundated with self-help books and information on how to be better, she has used her own story to empower others toward fulfilling their lives through their faith and using what they already have within them."

Shelly Brown, editor in chief of *Good Grit* magazine

"Eryn has devoted her life to helping people understand their worth. This book builds upon that legacy and takes a candid look at her own story. *So Worth Loving* reveals a profound understanding that our true humanity, our ability to love, is rooted in a God who first loved us."

Kurtis Johnson, first So Worth Loving employee,
friend, dad, and hot sauce enthusiast

SO WORTH LOVING

SO WORTH LOVING

how discovering your true value changes everything

eryn eddy

BakerBooks

a division of Baker Publishing Group
Grand Rapids, Michigan

Published by Baker Books
a division of Baker Publishing Group
PO Box 6287, Grand Rapids, MI 49516-6287
www.bakerbooks.com

Printed in the United States of America

Library of Congress Cataloging-in-Publication Data
Names: Eddy, Eryn, 1987– author.
Title: So worth loving : how discovering your true value changes everything / Eryn Eddy.
Description: Grand Rapids, Michigan : Baker Books, a division of Baker Publishing Group, [2021]
Identifiers: LCCN 2020036157 | ISBN 9781540900586 (paperback) | ISBN 9781540901538 (casebound)
Subjects: LCSH: God (Christianity)—Love. | Self-esteem—Religious aspects—Christianity. | Love—Religious aspects—Christianity.
Classification: LCC BT140 .E35 2021 | DDC 231/.6—dc23
LC record available at https://lccn.loc.gov/2020036157

The author is represented by The Bindery LLC.

21 22 23 24 25 26 27   7 6 5 4 3 2 1

To Craig and Juli Eddy,
informally known as Mama and Daddy:

You have weathered your own personal storms and selflessly stepped into mine without hesitation. God uses you as an instrument to show his love in people's lives, and mine is one of those lives. There are no words I could garner that would reflect appropriately my gratitude for you. I am honored and so proud that you are my parents. Thank you for never giving up on me.

CONTENTS

Foreword

I will never forget my first time meeting Eryn. I had followed her work through social media, and we had many mutual friends. From afar I admired her entrepreneurialism and passion to make the world a more hopeful place. Her kindness toward others was self-evident. Eryn's creativity and design were impeccable. Her compassion for the hurting was inspiring. When we finally connected in Atlanta, she blew me away.

Her energy and vulnerability were infectious. (By the way, you will find both of these things on every page of this book.) Everything I had heard and seen was true. She oozed positivity and her laugh sparkled. She was smart, wise, and fun. But what I most admired about her was her willingness to embrace the pain. She was able to sit in the tension of hope and personal suffering in such an inspiring way. I remember thinking to myself, *I wish more people were like her. The world would certainly be a better place.*

What I love about So Worth Loving and the words on these pages is that it is fully Eryn. It reflects exactly who she is and what she passionately believes in. It would be virtually impossible to miss her message, even if you don't feel so lovable right now. For many who read her words, you will want to be her best friend when you're done with this book. Actually, you'll most likely feel this way after just a couple paragraphs. And the reason is because she reflects back to us what we so often miss. Our value. Our goodness. That we are deeply loved even when we don't feel like it. And this is what a good friend does: they remind us who we really are. And Eryn is that friend.

She is unrelenting when it comes to breaking the shame that binds us. For her, these words and concepts are a way of life. When she reminds us that we are all "so worth loving," it's not a catchy slogan but an intervention. She is here to shake us from our slumber and wake us up to the power of radical grace in our lives.

Some authors write from a place of observation and kindly instruct us with tips and suggestions. Eryn takes a different approach. She pulls back all the personal protective layers and shows us the underbelly of the journey to actually knowing our true value. It is a road she has traveled in her own story. A story she has had to fight hard for. The beautiful nuggets of wisdom in this book ring true because she has lived through both the questions and the answers. She knows what it's like to carry something that we were not meant to carry. She writes as both a wise sage and a wounded warrior. This is what makes her words epic.

Shame and insecurity have hijacked too many of our stories. The pressure to hustle for our value has left us withered and deflated. The good news is, we don't have to live this way any longer. This marvelous book is the road map to help us get back to that place called love.

Mike Foster, counselor and host of
Fun Therapy podcast

Introduction

If you are like me, you never read introductions. But I promised my editor I would write one . . . so I gave it my best shot, and I think I actually like introductions now.

Why You're Here

If you're holding this book, you are most likely wondering if you are worth anything, wondering *Am I enough?* Maybe we are meeting in a season of life that feels a little heavy—maybe really heavy. Maybe you feel like you don't know what to do, where to go, who to trust, how you will get through, or who you are. Maybe your circumstance came out of nowhere, but here you are, and the uncertainty of it is pressing down on your chest.

After my divorce, I moved back home with my parents. I was about fifteen pounds underweight because my anxiety had diminished my appetite. I was depressed. My hair was falling out, and I barely brushed my teeth.

I was emotionally and physically exhausted.

I had been living in the hustle and bustle of Atlanta, Georgia. But then I found myself two hours away from there, back in my tiny hometown. I crawled into my parents' guest bed, still wearing all my clothes and makeup from the day. Lying there was the first time I truly acknowledged that I missed the presence of another person holding me at night.

Studies show that when someone holds you, your brain releases a happy chemical. For nine and a half years, I had a version of happy. But now, days were hard, and so was sleeping. I grabbed a king-size pillow to place behind my back, and I wrapped my arms around my body, hugging myself. I just wanted someone to hold me. I wanted someone to tell me I was going to be okay. After tossing and turning, I submerged my face into the pillow and bawled. Lipstick and eye makeup left an imprint on the pillow, not to mention more tears and snot than you can imagine.

I grabbed my phone to distract my mind and to try to regain myself. I scrolled through social media, checked my email, responded to a few text messages, and decided to open the Bible app on my phone. Maybe that would give me some relief. I mean, what do people do with so much grief and pain inside?

While I was pretty far from being engulfed in Scripture during that season, I entertained the passage of the day in hopes it would make me feel better:

> Are you tired? Worn out? Burned out on religion? Come to me. Get away with me and you'll recover your life. I'll show you how to take a real rest. Walk with me and work with me—watch how I do it. Learn the unforced rhythms of grace. I won't lay anything heavy or ill-fitting on you. Keep company with me and you'll learn to live freely and lightly. (Matt. 11:28–30)

I wanted a real rest. Looking back, I'm not sure my body had ever fully surrendered to a real rest. I wanted to recover my life. I was so worn out by a relationship, by work, by people . . . my self-respect was gone, and I didn't have a clue how to find it. I wanted to learn the unforced rhythm of God's grace. I wanted to live light and free, but after the death of my old life left me with a mountain of debt, that felt so far away. Really, I just wanted someone to keep me company. At that time, I wasn't sure it was God, but I was willing to think about it . . . I was willing to consider that maybe I could trust him and maybe he would give me some relief. But I was skeptical.

Are you a little bit skeptical like I was?

Are you tired? Tired of carrying things?

Are you burned out? Burned out from saying yes too many times?

Do you want to get away?

Do you want to recover your life?

Do you want to learn how to respect your heart again?

Do you want to experience real rest?

Do you want some company?

Maybe you just want to catch your breath. You just want a break.

Maybe you look around and realize it could be worse, but you still wonder, *Why does this confusion still feel so strong and overwhelming?*

A few things I want you to know . . .

You are not crazy.

You have permission to feel.

I'm glad you are here.

And yes, you are worth the fight.

It doesn't feel like it now, but it *will* be okay. *You* will be okay.

I hope you see this book as a formal journal. There will be a lot of asking questions and the beginning of finding some answers. This book contains the mistakes I've made and the boundaries I lacked. It carries the heartache of other people's decisions that ultimately made me very aware of my lack of self-worth. It also holds the things I've learned and the places I've grown.

Why Am I Writing This?

I'm sharing this battle of my heart because I don't believe I am alone in questioning and wondering, *Is God really present? What does he think of me? Does he hear me? Does he see me?* If you've ever felt like an underdog or an outcast, if you've ever felt like the uninvited or the lonely one, I know that feeling too.

This book is written from the place in my heart where the So Worth Loving movement began. A movement that started changing lives, including my own.

It's also written from the place in my heart where the light I'd prayed for when I was young had suddenly grown very dim. I didn't see through the rosy lens anymore. I went through a time of personal reckoning. If not for this reckoning, I wouldn't fully know or understand my true foundation and sense of worth. The beauty in the breakdown was finally seeing that the life I was living was a lie, and I had the opportunity to put things back together with truth.

So Worth Loving. It's not a fluffy, feel-good phrase. It truly is a lifestyle. It's about loving yourself. I'm not talking about being boastful or arrogant. I'm talking about the attributes of love. Treating yourself with patience, forgiveness, kindness, and gentleness. And treating others with patience, forgiveness, kindness, and gentleness.

As you learn to get to the other side, the side where your light will come back, you first have to accept where you are now. Your feelings are okay. Wherever you are today, it's important for you to know this: you are so worth loving.

The only shame that lives in these pages is the shame I've carried and want to share in hopes that it will help you feel less alone. So rest in knowing there will be no shaming and no judging here. No "You should haves." No "If you don'ts."

My heartbeat is for you to feel support and comfort through these words. For you to accept and embrace the joy, love, peace, patience, kindness, gentleness, and self-control inside of you right now. It is not a matter of "You might be worthy of love." You absolutely are, and we are going to explore and discover what got in the way of you believing that you are so worth loving.

This book won't give you ten steps to learning your self-worth or five ways to find your inner strength or the secret sauce to unlocking your power. If you came into this book hoping for that,

THE BEAUTY
IN THE BREAKDOWN
WAS FINALLY SEEING
THAT THE LIFE I WAS
LIVING WAS A LIE,
AND I HAD THE
OPPORTUNITY TO
PUT THINGS BACK
TOGETHER
WITH TRUTH.

you might want to pick up a different one. What this book will give you is a collection of my stories and revelations, the honest insights and struggles I've encountered in my pursuit of uncovering my worth.

I've made some poor choices in life; I've also made some bold decisions about moving forward and doing the best I can with what I know. After my choices left me battling a diminished sense of self-esteem and wondering if I had a purpose on this earth, I didn't have many places left to turn. So I took a chance and invited God in.

The words in this book found their roots in shaking, praying, and snot-crying. They found their roots in holy-surrendered ground but also in dark places where I was so far away from God. These words and the truth they hold only showed up when I silenced the noise around me and listened to God. I lived my way for far too long. Instead of facing the voids inside me, I filled them with external things. The load I carried was so heavy it made my knees buckle. I couldn't go any further. God came in and loved me back to life. The tender love with which he pursued me transformed my life. He showed me I was meant for more. He taught me that I am so worth loving, and even on the days I don't believe it, he knows it. He believes it.

After all my pursuits of instant gratification failed, after I'd exhausted all other options, I invited him in. I asked him to come close. He didn't care that he was my last resort. He welcomed me as if he were my first choice.

I started asking questions: *God, if you are real, if you are here, what do I need to know about you? What do I need to know about myself?* These questions led me to understand what it means to have a relationship with myself. And as I learned more about me, I developed a thirst to learn more about he who made me.

I believe the words in this book are from my Creator. The One who made me. He is my Hero when I so desperately need one. He is my Protector when I feel forgotten. He is my Guide when I feel so lost.

These words won't provide absolute answers to your questions, but I hope they will empower you to keep questioning, knowing that it brings you closer to God, not farther away from him. If you don't believe in God, I hope you don't let our differences impact our ability to connect. Pain is pain. Fear is fear. Heartbreak is heartbreak. Grief is grief. I have no motive other than to share. No matter our outlooks and beliefs, I know we can sit together and talk about our circumstances, our feelings, and what we are learning.

I'm thankful you are here. As you begin this book, I want to reiterate one thing: the desire to learn more about God did not just show up for me. I fought to see it prevail over my feelings and over the lies I was living out. I had to be really honest and repeatedly ask him to give me the energy to recommit my love to him.

Promise Me . . .

As you read, you will agree, disagree, tear pages out, read in a bubble bath, leave tear stains, take pen to paper, and underline, scratch out, and journal in the margins. You won't agree with everything I say. My experience is different than yours, and that is okay. But one thing we have in common is wrestling to discover what our true value is. And the truth is . . . you are valuable.

LOOK IN

---

becoming aware of what
is happening inside

I want to pray before we begin if that's okay . . .

If you're comfortable doing so, feel free to pray along with me:

*Lord, we come to you for protection over our thoughts and
relief over our circumstances.*

*Lord, we may feel tired but unsure how to tell you how
we feel. We may all be in different places in our lives right
now, but I do know you draw near when we invite you in.
Lord, our hearts may be jaded or hurt. We may be angry or
confused. We may not know how to talk to you. Will you
gently nudge us? To be gentle is to be able to relate, and
Lord, I know that's why you sent Jesus—to relate to us. To
know how we feel. You aren't scared of how we feel. I pray
we all will feel your presence. And I pray your presence will
overpower any fear or anger the enemy will attempt to bring
out as we look in. Looking in takes bravery and courage, and*

Lord, I believe you will respond to our bravery and courage by speaking up and speaking loud *as we begin to look into what our hearts are made of. I believe you will help us on our journey and help each person reading this understand that they are so worth loving.*

You are so good. And so loving. Thank you, Jesus, for your continual compassion. It's in your heavenly name we pray. Amen.

Where Am I Going?

"I can't get there."

Those four little words from the lips of a man I once kissed brought a relationship to an end and caused the baggage of my past to rush in. Those four little words revealed all the things I was trying to hide and peeled back the layers of pain in my heart I'd masked for many years. It took a painful breakup to release all the pressure bubbling up in my life. All the things I was running from. All the pain I was suppressing.

Leading up to those four little words, something just felt off. An uneasy, restless night turned into an unsettling morning as I waited anxiously for a call from the man I was seriously dating. By seriously, I mean we had met family and friends, integrated travel plans, celebrated holidays, joyfully introduced each other as the girlfriend or the boyfriend, and shared intimate moments, thoughts, and beliefs. When he finally called, I answered the phone, only to be crushed by those four little words: "Eryn, *I can't get there.*"

In an instant, it became all too apparent that despite the many therapy sessions I'd sat through, I still hadn't healed from my past trauma.

If you've ever been on the receiving end of those four little words or ones like it, you know the feeling. A flood of thoughts and questions, a surge of adrenaline, and panic. It's the fight, flight, or freeze moment . . . is it possible to do all three simultaneously? I certainly did.

After those four little words left the raspy voice I once longed to hear, I responded, "Get where?" He just kept saying, "I've tried to get there, but I just can't. We've reached a ceiling, and I can't get to where you need me to be in this relationship." My only expectation throughout the relationship was honesty about how he was feeling along the way, but instead, his quiet misleading suddenly left a painful residue on my heart.

I didn't put up much of a fight—partly because of shock, mostly because of pride. I didn't want to look like even more of a fool by begging him to stay. He started crying and I completely shut down.

After I got off the phone, I remember being flooded with so many questions and very few answers. I didn't believe him, yet I had to accept his choice. The words "I can't get there" were the equivalent of him saying, "I don't love you." Maybe he did, maybe he didn't, but right then and there, I told myself a lie. I told myself I was unlovable.

In an instant, all of our most intimate moments started playing in my mind. I felt used . . . hoodwinked . . . like I'd wasted my time on someone who could not just be honest with himself and honor me along the way. I started telling myself, *I'm inadequate, I'm not enough.* Yes, that was it . . . *I'm not enough.* If only I were more of this and less of that, *then* he would have stayed. Then he could have gotten "there," wherever *there* was.

I quickly fell into a shame spiral. Maybe you've experienced something similar. All my past pains returned, along with those nasty unanswered questions I had stuffed down for fear of what the answer might be: Will I confirm to my ex-husband all the terrible things he believed about me? And what about those people who judged me after my divorce? Did I prove them right too? Am I all those things they gossiped about me?

One year prior to this relationship, I had been married. My ex-husband and I were married for nine and a half years and together for thirteen years. We met when I was seventeen, got married when I was twenty-one, and were divorced by the time I was thirty. I did all the things a good Christian girl is supposed to do. I saved myself for marriage, completed premarital counseling, and as stubborn as I am, I *tried* to "submit to my husband." Ultimately, neither of us believed we were worthy of the love and freedom God unconditionally gives, which resulted in many hurtful actions, none of which are helpful for me to share here.

When I look back on my nasty shame spiral, I realize it did lead to one beautiful thing. It revealed the truth of what I thought about myself. When the truth is revealed and brought to light, it is rarely comfortable to observe. My shame spiral revealed the lies I'd agreed with and my truest feelings about myself. It shined a big bright light on how deeply I cared about what others thought of me.

While those words "I can't get there" crushed my heart, I realized shortly after . . . I couldn't get there either. I couldn't get to a place where I loved myself, which caused me to entrust my value and worth to another person. And to other people. I gave them the ability to validate me, to deem me as lovable and good. If I received their love, then I was good, I was loved, I was worth getting to know. But if I didn't, if I was rejected . . . shame spiral.

After the fateful phone call, I jumped in the shower and immediately sank to the floor. As I sat there, I couldn't distinguish between the stream of water and my streaming tears. I let them both wash over me, hoping they would wash away my thoughts.

But the feeling of rejection didn't have anywhere to go. I felt discarded. Thrown away. I felt denied. Sitting on my shower floor, the water felt like weights hitting the top of my head, pounding me with lies . . . if I was prettier, if I had better humor, if I was more cultured, I wouldn't have been rejected and denied. I asked the go-to question you ask when you're dumped . . .

What's wrong with me?

People have no dignity because they feel unloved. And they don't love & respect themselves.

You don't have to experience a breakup to ask that question. It can appear after the silence of a friend, or after turning in a résumé and not receiving a call back. It can appear after getting fired, or being outcast by your family. It can even surface all on its own, when no one says anything to you at all.

The breakup brought back the memory of when my family got in a car accident. Since my parents manufactured furniture, we spent lots of time on the road, going to furniture shows. We traveled with a giant trailer full of furniture attached to our car. As we trekked to a show in Pigeon Forge, I remember lying down in the third seat of the Suburban. My next memory is of hearing brakes squeal and feeling a jolt as we ran into the bumper of the tractor trailer in front of us. My seat folded in half and our luggage came flying forward.

The car accident provided a perfect analogy for my fallout from the breakup. The relationship folded in on itself, and all the baggage I had stuffed in the back came flying forward. It was excruciating. I wish I could say it was because we had something incredibly special, but the reality is, our unhealed, infected wounds caused the pain. We were two people feeling unloved, trying to find validation and love from each other, only to discover it wasn't there. And not even that it wasn't there, but that those four little words were true for both of us . . . "I can't get there."

After being crushed by the baggage from my past, I had nothing left to do except reflect on the healing that needed to happen and the pieces of my story I needed to own. I needed to explore why I cared so much about what other people thought. Was I codependent? Was I a narcissist? Was I self-absorbed? Maybe . . . I actually googled the definitions to all three things and then asked my therapist what he thought. He laughed and said narcissists don't ask, "Am I a narcissist?" Which provided a small amount of relief, but I still had the unanswered questions, *Why do I care so much about what people think? What is wrong with me?*

25

Over the next couple of months, with no real closure, I held out hope that my ex-boyfriend's name would appear on my phone and I'd hear him say, *"I made a mistake. I love you. I was just scared."* If he had, I could have gone back into hiding. I could have gone back to ignoring the things I needed to face. As awful as it sounds, in some ways he was just a mask, temporarily covering the painful things I didn't want to accept.

But he never called. I contemplated jumping back into the dating scene, thinking I could find another relationship. Since he wasn't the one, the one must still be out there. You know, the one who would pay attention to me, boost my self-esteem, shower me with affection, and show me I am worthy to be loved. But I didn't want to date anyone else. The idea made my stomach turn. Finally the tears stopped, and I accepted that he wasn't going to call. I needed to face who I was. Not who I thought I was but . . . who I really was.

Who Am I?

If you've ever been blindsided by the deconstruction of your life, you've probably asked yourself the same question, *Who am I?* When things suddenly fall apart, you step into a sudden awareness. And in that awareness, you recognize how your identity is attached to the very thing you lost, and now you ache because you realize you don't know how to answer that existential question. Sudden deconstruction leads to sudden awareness, and in the process, how you really view yourself is brought to light.

Unintentionally, we often find our identity in our circumstances, and when they take a dramatic turn, we're left feeling sad, embarrassed, alone, and confused. The dramatic turn could be a breakup, a custody battle, a sibling rivalry, or an abrupt end to a friendship; or failing school, filing for divorce, getting fired from a job, losing a business, facing financial hardship, or a million other things. But after it happens, we're left obsessing over what

Being a Mom!

we could have done differently, and depending on the devastation we are left with, we wonder if our lives will ever be normal again. Will we heal? Will we ever feel okay again? If we do, will that feeling be meaningful and real, or will we be timid and afraid, as if our joy and progress could be taken away again at any second?

As I stepped into awareness and became more honest with myself, I recognized that my need for a thriving relationship was just an effort to fill my inner void of loneliness. Deep down, I associated being whole with having a successful career and a thriving relationship. So, when I looked in the mirror after the end of another unhealthy relationship, with a pile of debt, the answer was clear: I was a nobody.

family
kids

Desiring a successful career or a thriving relationship isn't bad. In fact, they're both good. But the disconnect came because I was seeking those things to confirm that I was good and smart and worth loving instead of believing those things for myself.

After the breakup, I realized I didn't want to get to know me; I didn't even like spending time with me. I didn't have the relationship I wanted, and my finances were a mess, so there I was, against my choosing . . . cleanup crew of one.

But I had no idea how to start the cleanup process. If the way to feeling whole wasn't what I thought, then what did it mean to be whole? By definition, *whole* is healthy, complete, wholesome, free from damage. Could I ever be those things? Could I ever be healthy? Complete? Whole? Damage-free? I had a very long list of things that damaged my self-esteem. Damaged my sense of community and what I believed about relationships. How could I ever wriggle free from those things?

If we don't slow down long enough to be with ourselves, to look in and get to know ourselves, we won't ever be able to uncover what it means to be whole. But looking in is scary. It can make you want to run further away from yourself. If I'm honest, I tried a lot of quick-fix remedies before truly looking in and seeking to understand what it meant to be whole or how to get there.

YOU CAN'T CONTINUE PUTTING BAND-AIDS ON A WOUND;

YOU HAVE TO GIVE IT OXYGEN AND TIME.

Coming up with creative ways to bandage a wound might help conceal it, but it will never heal and become a scar. You can't continue putting Band-Aids on a wound; you have to give it oxygen and time.

I am so proud of what happened when I finally mustered up the courage to rip off the Band-Aid and look in. I acknowledged what was in there, who I was inside, and I learned how to love me, even in the middle of my pain. I learned to let go of outside opinions and to give myself grace. Awareness is messy, but awareness leads to discovering your true worth.

And that's what I want for you. So go ahead, when you're ready, rip off the Band-Aid, give it some oxygen. Let's start the healing process. Let's look in.

Agreement

agree·ment | \ə-ˈgrē-mənt\
the act of allowing or conforming

I was seven years old when I learned how semibelievable it was for me to act like Shania Twain and have my parents pretend to believe it. I was the last born of three girls, and because my sisters were six and eight years older, I was a real-life Barbie doll for them. If they wanted to dress me up, I was game. If they needed me to act in front of their camcorder, home movies were made. Dressing up and learning the lyrics to every Shania Twain song was a regular day in our home. My parents would often walk in on a music video set with my sisters pretending to direct our production.

Performing came at a young age for me, and performing for approval was also a part of the learning. I loved performing. I loved creating something that evoked emotion in someone else. If I could help bring out inspiration in someone, I had fulfilled a purpose. But at seven years old, I told myself I was accepted and loved because of the way I performed. What my sisters meant for no malicious intent whispered into my heart, and there began my agreement to a lie.

That lie continued to manifest over time: *If I perform well, you will love me. You will accept me. You will deem me good and worthy to know.*

When I was twelve, I had a karaoke machine, and I would make my entire family come down to the basement and watch me sing "Kiss from a Rose" by Seal. My sisters hated it because they were no longer the producers of the show, but also, since they were so much older than me, they had better things to do. Even if my parents had better things to do, they did not have the heart to leave in the middle of my performances. Mainly because of the effort I'd put into them. My performances did not stop with the karaoke machine. When I was sixteen, I started leading worship for a large church, and from there I grew in my performing. As I entered my twenties, I started to pursue a music career more seriously. I sang on large stages in front of thousands of people. I learned to gauge a room and respond based on what I saw expressed on people's faces.

At the time, social media was not the monster it is today. My generation was the beginning of that era. YouTube was the new thing for artists that Myspace used to be, and Tumblr was the new platform for online journaling—a platform that Xanga used to lead. As I started to produce music and put it out into the world on YouTube and Tumblr, I was not met with the kindness my parents had in our basement when I was young. I was met with critics who had no constructive criticism but only deconstructive attempts to tear down my self-esteem. I was told I was too skinny, I needed a spray tan, my voice was horrible, my lyrics were cheesy, I needed to be more of this or less of that. Then I'd be worth listening to. I'd be worth looking at. I'd be worthy of adoration.

And so I continued to feed the lie. The false statements others told me and I told myself became agreements in my life.

Had my seven-year-old self known that years later she would be the recipient of opinions from people who did not know her or her heart, I think she would have talked to herself differently. I think she would have decided her worth was not found in performing for other people's acceptance, and I don't think she would have lived by that false belief. I don't think she knew how to understand the truth of where her value could be found. While my parents did everything in their power to love my sisters and me well and accept us as we were, that still did not keep dark whispers away from planting a lie.

When I think back to my young age and the times I agreed with statements spoken over me, or when an uncomfortable silence would make its appearance after a nasty sibling fight, I remember quickly filling in the gaps with the conclusion that I was the problem and that I just hadn't performed well enough that time to be loved.

And truthfully, at that young age I did not know how to determine where my worth should or should not be found, for I saw results instantly when I performed, and those results seemed valid. I was learning by the response of others, and it felt like love when I did things right. With applause came feeling accepted, and feeling accepted deemed me lovable. Performing was a counterfeit of love, and still sometimes that counterfeit feels more real than what true love is.

Can you think back to when you were young and pinpoint a lie that became something you agreed with and lived out? Maybe you are the oldest of a large family, and the only way you were seen or acknowledged by your parents was if you were in turmoil. If your life was chaotic, you actually felt seen and loved. Attention was your counterfeit love. Maybe you told yourself, *You are loved if you have immense pain to share.* Or maybe you agreed with your dad when he expressed that beauty was a sin. Beauty was arrogance. So you rejected any form of external beauty, whether it was the way you dressed or took care of your skin or did your hair. Because who wants to be arrogant? I mean, if that were true, who would want to be a physical example of sin? The birthplace of our agreements is understandable, and there is no shame in what you believed, but I want to encourage you to identify the things you agreed to that became beliefs you started to live out.

[handwritten margin note: not worthy of friendships, feeling of rejection/divorce]

33

Maybe you had a sibling who told you that you were only worth loving if you agreed with them, and so you learned to conform to other people's opinions to feel loved, and over time you didn't know how to confidently have a voice. Maybe your parent never hugged you or told you that you were beautiful, so you told yourself you weren't deserving of affection or attention. Or maybe the complete opposite—you went running toward any guy who would give you affection and attention. Whatever it is, you made an agreement, silenced your voice, and coasted on autopilot.

More rejection

You may have made an agreement to carry the shame from your past mistakes, your longing to change your relationship status, the career path you chose, or your family history. More tangibly, the results of these agreements can take the form of rejecting the way you're made, normalizing a relative's abuse, giving your body to different guys, overachieving in your career for validation, or being gaslighted by a spouse due to their addiction.[1]

Recognizing your agreements is scary because being honest about them means work, and if life is already hard, why would we purposely make it harder? We may find ourselves closing our eyes and hoping that if we keep moving forward, our negative inner voice will disappear and go away. Unfortunately, as much as I wish the things I agreed to didn't create more problems, ignoring them infected my entire belief system about who I was and how to receive love. Eventually, these agreements showed their ugly faces to me. The first time I really understood what I had been agreeing to was when I went to therapy.

If you have been to therapy, you know what I am talking about when I share that it was *awkward*. If you have never been to therapy, this may be the reason you haven't been. Because it will be *awkward*. There is this uncomfortable exchange for at least the first three visits before it gets kind of comfortable. You likely do one of two things on those early visits: either you tiptoe into

1. Gaslighted: manipulated by psychological means into questioning your own reality.

your story for fear of judgment and gasps, *or* you lay it all out within fifteen minutes and then walk away feeling like a complete basket case.

I am no stranger to therapy. I started going fourteen years ago. I was twenty years old and engaged at the time. During my first visit, I became aware of something controlling my life: fear. I was so fearful. Specifically, I was fearful of death, and I had the realization that my fiancé was going to die one day. In that session, I treated the fear topically. I dealt with the symptoms but not the root. My therapist helped me accept that uncertainties happen in life and we won't physically die from the emotional pain that comes with the acceptance that life is fragile and someone we love might die unexpectedly. She would say, "What would you do?" and I would answer. She would say, "And then what would you do?" and I would answer . . . and I would find myself walking down the hallway of fear to learn that, while pain would come, I would be okay.

For years, I went to talk with a therapist about the dysfunction of my family, and thankfully, I learned every family has dysfunction. But more specifically, I went to seek guidance for an unhealthy dynamic I had with a sibling. Again, I treated my symptoms topically. I would go to therapy for a specific circumstance, and when I got done with that circumstance, we would discuss another one. I thought to myself, *I am a pro at this, and there isn't much I don't know about me . . .*

The scary thing about thinking you are a pro at anything is that the moment you think you are not susceptible to something is often the moment you're the most vulnerable to it.

What I learned was that, while I could treat my circumstances topically in therapy, I wasn't facing any of my deeply rooted agreements. Treating the circumstance was a lot like treating the symptom of a terrible infection. I struggled to get to the root because, honestly, I was scared to admit what I had agreed to about myself. If I exposed the lie, would that make me more unlovable? I started to believe that this agreement, this lie, kept me safer than the truth.

In my genuine attempt to face things in therapy, I found that I was more interested in fixing circumstances quickly so I would appear healthy than facing things that were hiding deep down. I've often heard it said that during pressure we see what is in our heart.

During my divorce, all my agreements came out. There was no way of escaping what I had believed about myself. My therapist often shared with me that our thoughts become beliefs and our beliefs become our actions. If we believe we need to perform for love, inevitably our choices will reflect that. So, naturally, no matter how hard I suppressed them . . . my agreements came out, not in a safe therapy session but in my response to people around me during my divorce. I believed lies and then told lies. I lied to people about the pain I had been enduring. I lied about the choices I made. I lied to protect the unhealthiness occurring in my home. I wanted so badly to appear healthy. After my divorce, my agreements led to a lifestyle that entailed late nights out, taking shots in bars, and dating the wrong types of guys. These agreements came out in how I spent my money, and they came out in the type of friend I struggled to be.

I believed a lie, lived a lie, then watched the town make up more lies. I felt so confused about what was true. I had "friends" who wanted to meet up with me to learn the truth about why my life appeared to be unraveling, but I was in so much denial I could not give them a truthful answer.

Agreements felt like truth because I had lived in them for so long. I was one giant construction zone and I needed to get to work. As I went to work on trying to understand the difference between what was true and what wasn't, I learned that old ways don't die fast. I had twenty-two years of suppressed agreements.

When I started to acknowledge this construction zone of agreements, the only thing I could think to do was to disappear. Maybe that would silence the noise. I moved to the country and back in with my parents. People talked about my leaving town, but I had only roughly four visitors in two years after moving from a community I'd invested seven years into. The silence of others only added to the loud whispers I was trying to quiet.

Keeping quiet about what you have agreed to is not the same as learning what your agreements are in quiet.

And while moving north of the city to clear my head was an understandable attempt to handle what was happening, I had not killed the underlying agreements that had brought me to this. I maintained them. I went to social media to demonstrate I was stronger, healthier, and happier. And while that was half true, a half-truth is still a lie. I wasn't healthier, but for the first time, I desired to understand myself to the core—to understand what healthy meant. In that time, living on my parents' property in the country, I learned that silence was a gift. An uncomfortable gift that showed me who was a friend and who wasn't. And this gift of silence showed me what was buried inside me: what I really thought of myself and what I had agreed to.

In order to mend a broken heart and bring the right friends, family, therapists, and God into these spaces, we must identify where we have been giving parts of our heart to the wrong places. To understand where we need to go, we need to know our old ways won't get us there. We are on a new path. I understand it's excruciating to be that vulnerable with anyone, let alone God. During the time when everything went quiet, I questioned if he was even around. Did he see me making all those agreements and not care? Your idea of God might have been that he is a punisher and will cause harm to you if he hears what you've done or what you think. If you grew up in a Christian household like I did, you could just be so numb to Christian verbiage that it no longer has meaning to you. Or it could be that the words you have been around in your Christian faith were used as weapons to control you rather than tools to comfort you. Maybe you were like me and mistook Christians' views as the same views God has of you.

I want to express that I'm so sorry that you may feel alone in wrestling with the inner lies as you face the weight of your agreements. I want to give you hope that you will come out of this, and when you do, you will have a deeper compassion for people who feel alone just like you did.

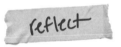

- Identify the lies you have quietly agreed to. Are there specific words you tell yourself that you know deep down don't reflect who you are? For example,
  » I'm not pretty enough.
  » I'm not smart enough.
  » If only I were more of ____, then _____ would happen.
- Journal where your mind goes when you are silent. Sometimes these lies are hard to identify until we silence everything around us. Write down what comes to mind.
- Replace agreements with truths. If you are unable to combat the agreements, text a safe friend or mentor and ask them to help you replace the agreements with truths. Write down these truths and place them where you'll see them daily:
  » Tape them to your mirror, on your fridge, and next to your sink.
  » Set reminders on your phone and desktop to pop up throughout the day.

Reflection

re·flec·tion | \ri-'flek-shǝn\
the return of a likeness or image as in a mirror

When I was young, I visited the doctor more regularly than most little girls did. My body mass index was never on the same path as what is considered healthy or average. I was told by health care professionals that I was below average and likely always would be.

I am sure you can relate to comparing yourself to images on billboards, magazine covers, social media posts, and Pinterest of women who don't look like you. You may have agreed with the message from society that you see on a daily basis that those women are prettier. Sexier. Slimmer. Curvier. That if you were more of this and less of that, you would be accepted and valued. Whether you compare yourself or you have been in a relationship with someone who compared you to a standard, you and I most likely share the same mirror, despite our shape and size. A mirror that says we should look a certain way or we are not enough.

During those visits to the doctor, my mom would do her best to respond to the doctor's concern for my lack of growth while trying to affirm there was nothing wrong with me. We couldn't quite figure out why I was *this small*. More doctors' visits and a lot of blood work and examinations only confirmed I was, and would always be, below average. My body would have no chance of competing with a 5'7" model; I would be 4'11", maybe 5'1" with heels.

Growing up, I got used to the questions people asked. When I was introduced to someone, my size was the first thing people noticed. I often heard, "Do you ever eat? You should eat two burgers for dinner. Do you have a disease? Have you visited the North Pole recently? Can I put you in my pocket? I just want to put you on my shelf."

I remember one particular instance when a relative introduced me: "This is Eryn. Don't worry, she doesn't have an eating disorder; she's just small." And whether I did or didn't have an eating disorder, that statement was full of so much shame. If I did, is that how we handle the way we see someone? And if I didn't, again, is that how we handle the way we see someone? As much as we may be concerned about the way we look, there will always be people who have opinions too. So, how do we live our life out of a truthful lens?

Over time, instead of hearing those statements and replacing them in my mind with truth, I just got used to them, and I also got pretty resentful of them. Instead of the words sliding off like beads on a Rain-X windshield, I would let the downpour of the rain disrupt my view of myself.

At twenty-two, I decided to *finally* get to the bottom of what was going on. I remember sitting at the doctor's office believing I had found a doctor who could confirm there was something wrong with me, and I could finally have the answer. When someone asked, "So, are you always going to be this small?" I could say, "Yes, and to ease your mind, here is a scientific reason why."

This was a naturopathic doctor who had been an internal medicine doctor for twenty years at Emory Hospital. *This woman knows what's up,* I thought, *and she will tell me what no doctor could for the last twenty-two years.*

After an exam and blood work, she grabbed my petite wrists and she said to me, "Eryn, I want you to look at your wrist. You see your bones? You were made like this on purpose. There is no cure for your size and there is nothing wrong with you. This is you."

In an instant, I was changed from that visit. When people would ask why I was so small, I would now have an answer: I'm built this way on purpose. Don't we all want that relief? Someone to say, "Hey, you were built this way on purpose." Sure, we can improve our health, take better care of our bodies, and tend to ourselves properly, but wouldn't it be nice if we could silence the discomfort that others have about our bodies and say, "You know what? This body I reside in was built this way on purpose. While society says it's below average, my God says it's on purpose."

I never used to talk about my struggles with my body. I would ignore them because I'd often hear statements like "Well, at least you're small" or "You should see it as a blessing, Eryn." I didn't talk about my struggles because I felt they were invalid. I think we do that with our feelings too, right? We say, *Well, someone has it worse,* but if we silence our struggles, they will never be tended to, and if we don't tend to them, they will grow into something bigger. Lies manifest in secret, and our actions will eventually reflect the lies more than the truth.

Someone out there is going to say you are not right. Someone out there may have told you that you are below average. They may have even told you that you are not even close to the standard. Whether you feel you are too small or too big, you have told yourself you are just not right. You've believed your body does not have a purpose because it does not meet the expectations that have been placed on you. It doesn't matter if it's a doctor who tells you or a friend or a stranger. I am going to tell you now, we have a responsibility to take care of our body. To treat it with kindness, respect, integrity, and honor, and not just because of health reasons but because it is the instrument used to fulfill our purpose. No one can impact the world like you can. You have unique gifts that only you are carrying in that frame of yours. We are meant to discover and accomplish above-average work. If we keep telling

YOU WERE MADE LIKE THIS ON PURPOSE.

ourselves we are below average, how will we ever get to a place of valuing and honoring ourselves and holding to the belief that we were made on purpose?

We can spend our entire life searching for what others think is right, or we can decide what is right and learn to rewire our minds to believe the truth from the source that made it. God made us this way, he accepts us as we are, and he offers us the opportunity to see ourselves the way he sees us. When we embrace his loving view of us, all other opinions become less important. I'm thirty-three, and for the first time, I am finally embracing that I am built like this on purpose. I don't look thirty-three. People ask me all the time if I'm in college, and it's honestly somewhat embarrassing to go into the kids' department to pick out pants that will fit me. It's not necessarily an enjoyable shopping experience. I used to loathe shopping for clothes because I was constantly reminded when trying things on that I'm not an acceptable size, and I think you can relate to me on this, right? An image from an advertisement will flash in front of my eyes, and I'll compare what I see in the mirror to what I've seen on social media.

It is a continual battle for me to accept that I was made on purpose, but I was, and I have a purpose. And I will fight the battle to believe it, with God as the Protector of my mind, and any time those thoughts pop up, I will say, "God, will you speak up when I look in? Will you speak up when I start to listen to other people's voices above yours?"

Have you had a hard time looking in the mirror? Do images of what you consider ideal flash in front of you when you do? Do you wonder if maybe you would not be single if you looked a certain way? Or maybe you thought you were beautiful until you dated or married someone who wanted to change your image. Do you wonder if you would be appreciated more if you wore different clothes or if your tummy didn't bulge out as much? Our not-so-kind answers to these little questions lead to agreements we make about ourselves to complete a narrative of our story. But I want to propose that there might be places in yourself you haven't loved yet. <u>You may have had to come unglued to see the pieces that needed healing, the parts of you that needed forgiveness.</u> You may need to forgive yourself for the way you talk to your body, and you may need to forgive others for the way they talk about how you look or dress. While I am not advocating that in order to accept yourself, you can't dress in a way that feels cute, apply makeup, or dye your hair, I am advocating for being really honest with the words you say to yourself about why you do those things. <u>Tough love is good—it's healthy—but destructive words are not love.</u>

We can choose to do the work, understanding that it will feel like a shedding of our old self. There are places inside you that you haven't loved yet, so lean in and ask God to speak up when you look in.

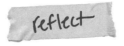

Let's do a heart check. How do you see yourself? Through the eyes of others? Have you borrowed opinions of what others think about you? If your heart beats to fear, shame, or doubt, I understand the uncomfortable feeling you may have. I know all too well the pain of acknowledging damaging words you have said to yourself. In one of my darkest nights, during my deepest heartbreak, I admitted how I felt about myself, placing my hand over my heart and praying, "God, hold my heart; it hurts so bad. Protect this heart. You are my Protector. <u>Replace my thoughts with yours.</u>"

Lord, I pray for peace and protection over our thoughts. We know the enemy wants to keep us in a space of fear, but that is not of you. You are love. You are peace. You are patience and kindness and rest. I pray for protection and rest over our tired souls. I pray that we will feel your loving arms wrapped around us. I pray that our homes may be filled with only your presence. I pray that we may know and understand that you are the source of love and never the source of fear—you are not a shaming, condemning God. You desire that we live a life of light, not darkness. I pray for the person who is currently experiencing a lot of darkness, that they may see the purpose and beauty that come from it and that you will show them those glimpses as they continue to be refined for the road you have set for them. Amen.

Unfinished

un·fin·ished | \ən-ˈfi-nisht\
left unacknowledged or unaddressed

When we begin to look inside ourselves, we are faced with things we have yet to address, our unfinished work. Or maybe I should say work we abandoned, were too scared to acknowledge, or in my case, left unfinished due to denial. I want to be careful with discussing the work we need to face, because here's the thing: we won't ever arrive to completion while we are on this earth. There will always be unfinished work. However, the amount of focus we put into our work will determine the quality of life and relationships we have. When we pay attention to what is going on inside of us, not only will we reap the benefits of that hard work but so will our friends and families.

The unfinished, unfaced work may be a result of temptations we caved in to that left us feeling worse or indulgences we don't want to let go of. Our unfinished work stays unfinished because instant gratification gets in the way. We may acknowledge the issue we need to work on but resort to a temporary solution, perpetuating the behavior and never really coming close to completing the work. We might even say to ourselves, *It's fine. It feels good*, but could the instant relief that makes us feel better be true? Could

46

it last? Man, I wish. Facing unfinished things would be a heck of a lot easier.

Some people are closer than others to doing the work needed on their hearts, but there is one important thing we must remember: not to compare our journey to theirs. In order to acknowledge unfinished business, we must first be present enough in our life to see it. But here is the kicker: we must *want* to see the unfiltered reality so badly that the temptation to deny it is not even an option. If you're uncomfortable or unfamiliar with blatant truth, then this will feel like a scary beginning to the unveiling of the beliefs you have about yourself. Sometimes the truth is hard to look at, but *truth* is the one thing that will set us free. It's the one thing that breathes oxygen on those wounds that need to heal. Deep down, the unfinished work we need to do can be difficult for us to examine, whether our self-esteem is fragile or our pride is strong.

During my separation, I didn't tell many people what was going on. The only people who knew my husband and I were separated were the couple I was staying with and my therapist, but news got out and it got out quickly. In a city where we were both connected to everything and everyone, it was only a matter of time. Maybe I was too trusting to think that kind of news would be tended to carefully.

To escape from it all, I would go to a taco joint and do my work from there. I didn't want to be home, and I didn't want to be at work. I was surrounded by things I wasn't ready to face, and this taco joint felt like a temporary vacation. The waitstaff was so kind to me—maybe a little too kind. I was a regular, and I wasn't above taking shots with the bartender. While in some ways it was a relief, in other ways it was an escape. One day, I was meeting someone I considered to be a close friend, and that evening, she confronted me about the news that my husband and I were separated. I said, "Yes, we are," not knowing where to even begin my explanation. I hadn't let many people—let alone myself—into my story. I had vacated my own story before everything came to the surface, and

I maintained that absence. It was too painful to face why the separation was suddenly happening. My friend expressed that she was shocked. She said she had been checking in on my social media to see how I was doing and everything looked fine. I think we can recognize a few problems with this conversation and the direction it was headed. One, I clearly was not as engaged in my life as I was in my social media, and two, she was more engaged with my social media than she was with me.

Don't you find it crazy that we live in the most socially connected era? At our fingertips, we have immediate access to each other at any point of the day, yet the night comes, and we feel so alone. The lives of those around us have much deeper things going on than we know. They, too, have unfinished work and are often degrees away from admitting it and tending to it. More likely than not, they are escaping from having to see it. I think that is why you can see a photograph of a friend on social media, and the caption, the outfit, the smile, and the color of their filter promise that they are doing great, that they are at their all-time best season of life, and yet you may know the truth of what is going on internally. You may know personally that they are actually in the darkest season of their life, but they are so scared to look at it, they look to their social media to escape. It is a common temptation to color our circumstances with a temporary relief. Any form of relief gives us hope, and that is ultimately what we want . . . something to hope for. We hope things will get better. If we speak it out, surely it will come true . . . but the problem is, we have a lot of megaphones speaking out and not a lot of hands that are willing to get dirty in their own work.

Maybe the work has stayed unfinished due to fear of the unknown, the paralyzed state that a betrayal has left you in, or guilt from your choices. Shame will lie to you and try so hard to convince you that you are your choices. Or maybe the work is unfinished because you have been able to mask it to help you escape.

Don't get me wrong, I love filters, design, art, color tones (if you think I didn't have a lot of input in this book cover, you're wrong) but I hope we don't let these things trick us into believing our circumstances are fixed just because we've made them look good. I'm not saying we should air out all our deepest, darkest pain on social media. Maybe what I am suggesting is that we put down our phones and resist the way we color our lives so that we may become more aware that the likes and comments only give us temporary relief. We don't owe anyone on social media all the details of what we are going through; however, we do owe it to ourselves to actually face the things that bubble up, and the only way to do that is to stop seeking the applause and become familiar with silence. I can't help but think we spend more time with our heads down, editing our reality instead of looking in and accepting the reality of our life.

While our social media presence increases, our actual physical presence in our own life and in the lives around us decreases. While we are busy capturing moments, we are actually forgetting moments or, maybe even worse, not experiencing them in the first place. We get so involved in how to portray our reality that we don't focus on actually living in it.

The longer we avoid what's really going on, the longer we have places inside us that remain abandoned, deteriorating every bit of contentment, joy, confidence, independence, and sense of worth we may have had.

Do you wish you were happier? Do you wish you could have that contagious joy? Do you feel weighed down by choices you've made? Do you feel the sting of harsh judgment from a friend that you can't shake? All the things we feel we lack, and all the sadness we carry into a room, are a reflection of our core belief. What we believe about ourselves and what we believe about God.

We have to acknowledge that we have made agreements with lies we've been told about ourselves. Acknowledge we have unfinished work because of them. Acknowledge some things need to be uprooted and brought to light—things we thought we'd handled, things we allowed to stay quiet, things we covered with something else. There is work to be done, and if we don't gently walk toward it, it will inevitably bubble up and show itself without our choosing. It's not a matter of if but when. Unfinished work looks a lot like unforgiveness, a lie lived out, or not reconciling with statements that were made about you. Identifying unfinished work is the beginning of looking in and the end of our striving for perfection. It's a brave step into the reality of how you see yourself.

At that low-lit taco restaurant with my friend, I realized I could not really share with her the work, or lack of work, in my life because I was scared to see it. I also did not want to bring to light what had been buried and in the dark. I did not want to uproot it, especially in a place that I used as an escape.

Uprooted

There was a tree on my parents' property that I always thought was beautiful and so full of life. It had long, strong branches and foliage filled every nook of it. It was the kind of tree you dreamed of climbing to the top of. The kind of tree that gave the gift of allowing you to see the whole world ahead of you—to see and to dream. The kind of tree in which you felt protected, where no harm from the ground could get to you. You could see views that only this tree offered. It was steady to the sun as it was to the moon.

I can recall coming home to visit my parents one day to find that the tree had suddenly been uprooted.

It lay on its side, hugging the soil as if it were whispering to the ground, the only thing close to it, *Why am I not greeting the sun and moon anymore?*

What once was a beautiful, admirable fixture that offered protection, safety, and life, lay down in devastation. Something had impacted this tree. Whether it was a storm, waterlogging, age, an infestation, or lack of nutrients, it had no other option but to lie there as nature continued to evolve around it.

It seemed the tree was grieving as it lay on one side looking around at its now limited view. It was as though the tree noticed that not one thing around it had been impacted directly by its being uprooted.

Do you see yourself as that tree? I did.

I felt as though my life had flipped upside down and my identity, worth, and self-esteem were uprooted for everyone to see once I was honest with what my roots were made of. I was full-on hugging the ground. Hugging the ground just like that tree . . . not wanting to be on the ground but being crippled by my thoughts and saying to myself, *Maybe this is where I should stay.*

I watched other people's lives continue on while it felt like mine had shrapnel spread throughout every part of it. My personal life was a disaster, and that disaster leaked into my business. My lack of boundaries and my insecurities were displayed for all to see. I felt a hit from every corner. Have you ever experienced that?

I was once a woman full of laughter and life, and I slowly began to turn into someone I did not know. I began to wonder when I would laugh again, just as the tree seemed to wonder if it would see the sun the same way again.

I'm sure you've seen a tree that's been completely uprooted. It looks like Goliath came by and plucked it out of the ground, and all the roots that kept it stable are now saying hello to the sky for the first time. Those roots are probably wondering why they are not operating at their innate function and why all of nature is seeing them so vulnerable in the light. Instead of the top of the tree seeing the sun, now the roots are. There is a gaping hole left exposed in the foundation for anything and everything to get inside and peek into the darkness where the roots used to be planted. Just as what's left of this beautiful tree has creatures looking inside, you, too, are most likely looking into your own life. You might even have friends, family, or acquaintances who feel entitled to look and speak into the situation because it's visible from the outside.

Did you know that a tree that has been uprooted can in fact be reintroduced to the soil to have another life? With proper care, it can come back to life and live anew. There is also something called a tree graft. A tree can be planted into an old tree, creating a bond for a new life to grow.

Just as a tree has roots that store and supply nutrients and serve as the anchor to keep the tree steady and strong as it grows, so do we have roots that keep us grounded in our foundation. But what is the health of that foundation? What kind of nutrients have we been feeding it? What do we tell ourselves? What do we absorb from others?

Over time we will see the result of the nutrients we have absorbed from everything we have consumed. This will either enhance or deteriorate our foundation. When we do not tend to ourselves with proper care, we may find ourselves lying down in circumstances we could have prevented.

Of course, some things are out of our control, but we can control how we react and what we feed our roots after an expected or unexpected implosion. We may not be able to control our circumstances, but we can ask ourselves, *Are we prepared?*

With the much-needed attention to our roots, we can live a healthier, more fruitful life because we've taken the time to care for the areas that make up our foundation. Some of that involves being uprooted and exposing what's hidden to the light.

Matthew 15:13 (CSB) says, "Every plant that my heavenly Father didn't plant will be uprooted."

Let this be our prayer: *Lord, uproot the things you do not want in my life.* This prayer can feel scary, but it is the very prayer that will reveal the things in you that need healing. That thing you resist talking to him about might be the thing he uproots. It is your choice to believe his way is better than yours. Rarely is this a convenient prayer. Rarely do we like God answering it, but when he does, we see that his response is protection. Anything planted that is not supposed to be there is harmful, and it's only a matter of time before you will see the result of it.

Be Prepared for the Results of Your Bold Prayers

I started to do the work. Uprooting things. Rebuilding my life. I wanted God involved in everything because I was so desperate to not be that tree lying on the ground forever. I prayed a bold prayer one week before a business deal that had been in the works for six months was expected to be finalized. This deal was going to offer so much relief. It was going to give me the support I had been longing for as a lonely entrepreneur. Within one week of that prayer, everything fell through. God shut it down. Completely. What I had been negotiating with another company for six months ended in two phone calls after that prayer. God *shut it down*. God simply said, "I see your heart; I want protection for you. What's not of me, I will remove because you invited me in." And he did.

After the two phone calls, I was so confused and honestly heartstruck. *Why?!* I had been working so hard on this. I had been positioning my life for this new transition. I asked God, "What did I do wrong? Why did this happen?" I went even more extreme, asking God, "Do you not want me to work for my company anymore?" And then I remembered the prayer. That bold, heart-all-in kind of prayer.

God had answered my prayer. It was nothing I did wrong but what I did right. I prayed and trusted that God was going to remove and move anything out of my life that was not of him. He did just that. So, while we pray as things in our life are being uprooted, may we also pray that whatever is planted *is* of God. Is of his love. There was so much in my life to uproot because I had planted things without any of his involvement, and while he can make things beautiful that were meant to keep us lying on the ground, eventually things that were not supposed to be planted in the first place will be uprooted.

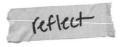

- Identify what needs work. What needs to be uprooted?
  - » Pray and ask God to remove and move anything that is not good for you.
  - » Pray and ask God to give you strength and affirm that you are good as he removes what needs to be gone from your life.
- Take a break from social media.
  - » Set parameters on what you are consuming while being honest with yourself about what to uproot. We can feel pretty low when we compare our lives to those of others, seeing all the things we aren't involved in or wishing we had what they have. Let's stop a spiral before it begins.
  - » Give yourself grace and remember to take deep breaths from your diaphragm as you do the difficult work of facing what's hidden and allowing God to uproot what does not belong.

Heavy

heav·y | \'he-vē\
hard to bear

Have you ever seen one of those vintage suitcases? The rectangular retro-looking kind that do not have wheels? I bought one online, and it was beautiful. It was from the 1940s, light blue, with a vintage pinstripe. The interior was even more beautiful, with a plaid lining. I romanticized the idea that when I traveled, I would look different from everyone else. I showed up at the airport with my suitcase looking like I was ready for Paris. I was not going to Paris. In fact, I was going to Texas. Not even remotely close. Can I tell you, that suitcase was the worst, most impractical purchase I have made?

While I had packed light, knowing I would be carrying rather than rolling the suitcase, the longer the stretch to security was, the more I noticed how weak my upper-body muscles were. I did not want to look like a fool carrying it, so I held it close to my body and prayed inside, *God, get me to the gate. My arm feels like it is bleeding and going to fall off*. Unfortunately, my arms got tired, and before I could take one more step, I dropped everything, the suitcase popped open, and all of what I'd been carrying was displayed for everyone to see. It did not matter if people were going in different directions, they stopped and stared to see what was inside, what I had been carrying around. I think of it this way: my trendy vintage suitcase was carrying all my agreements and unfinished work that I had not yet opened. As much as I wanted to pretend I could carry all that weight, I simply could not. More often than not, I think we do that without even realizing it.

Oh yeah, by the way, my little arms took a week to recover from lugging that suitcase around, so after that, it served as a place in my house to store books for a while before I eventually took it to a thrift store. That suitcase only dreamed of traveling to Paris.

Sometimes we carry more weight than we are designed for, and even if we make it look easy, we feel alone and heavy inside. We are afraid to face the things inside of us, and we don't leave the door open for others to help us face them. If we are to love others well, we must learn to love ourselves and what we consist of. The good, the bad, the light, the heavy.

While we may believe we are prepared, when life throws a curveball, we either crumble, deny it, or get stronger. We need to lighten our expectations of ourselves when we are dealing with heavy things. We are complex, and we are learning more and more every day how to extend acceptance and approval to ourselves and our story.

I used to be one who did not like to sit in her pain. I didn't like to see it or feel it. I would pretend it wasn't there most of the time. However, if someone else was in pain, I was the friend they called when they were ready to be encouraged and see the bright side of things. I guess you could say I was the pep talk they were looking for when they were ready for gentle questions and optimism.

So, you can imagine how I handled it when my life was completely dismantled. When I had debt collectors calling me, a recent divorce to my name, a career that was on pause, a breast cancer scare, my father's diagnosis of throat cancer, and—to top it off—I was the subject of the town's gossip. I drank a lot and flirted with guys a lot. I was not very fun to be around because I didn't even want to be in my own story. When I saw friends, I either repeated stories they already knew about how unhappy and depressed I was and why it was valid that I felt that way, or I put on a mask and denied my circumstances. Whether I was spewing it out or holding it in, both approaches felt heavy—for the recipient and for me. And I didn't know there could be a balance.

Oftentimes, we keep what we are carrying quiet for fear someone will judge it and tell us we aren't worthy of the very thing we desire. We want redemption, to be recovered and found as loved. In my spewing and in my hiding, I just wanted to know that I'd be okay and that I could be loved no matter what was going on in my life. I wanted to believe that my circumstances didn't define me.

My therapist reminded me that I must grieve. To lighten the load of all we have been carrying does not mean we ignore it, and it also does not mean we share it with everyone to get it off our chest. To lighten our load when it's heavy means we have to grieve. We have to grieve what we thought our story was going to be and surrender to and accept what it is becoming.

While I am not my circumstance, my circumstance has enabled me to develop into the woman I am now. My capacity to feel, express, and sit with pain is far deeper than it would be if I never went through a hard, life-altering experience.

Some circumstances in our lives won't have a cherry on top after we get to the other side. Some of them might actually stamp on our hearts and minds a perpetual grief that we must move forward with . . . but the sliver of beauty we will find is that the depth of pain we allow ourselves to feel and see may benefit someone else who is scared to face theirs. It will give hope. If you allow it, your story will be an offering to help bring someone through their lowest moments.

Hello. Hi. While I haven't had a chance to have a conversation with Adele about this yet, I read in an article that her song "Hello" was not a brokenhearted love song about a relationship with another person but a brokenhearted love song about a relationship with her younger self. She sings, "Hello, it's me. I was wondering if after all these years, you'd like to meet."

Can you look back on your life and see areas you've abandoned? Can you see all the space between where you used to be and where you are now? For me, that abandonment looked like neglecting myself: quieting my personality so I wouldn't be too much or silencing my thoughts and opinions on something that mattered to me. Abandonment was losing my independence and becoming codependent to another person's point of view. Abandonment was extinguishing a healthy desire to be close to God because I was uncomfortable with a relationship I was allowing myself to be in with someone else. Abandonment was caring too much about what others thought and being willing to neglect what I thought.

For you, abandonment could be losing all the sweet and special things that made up your personality or the things that kept your naïveté safe. Maybe you realized the world is not as sweet as you thought, and maybe you lost your way in it. Maybe you recognized the abandonment of yourself when everything was uprooted. Or you look back on all the little losses you hadn't grieved but had instead suppressed because it felt silly to give them any light, yet maybe the longing is deep in you for them to get some air.

Those reflections are painful. That loss of naïveté and awareness of abandonment are things to mourn as much as they are things to accept. Time does not heal as much as awareness does, and the awareness of our circumstances gets us closer to healing the areas we've abandoned.

If you have abandoned your joy, you'll get your laughter back, and that laughter will have much more soul and meaning because you now have an appreciation of what you neglected.

With the growth you gain in your healing, you won't have that naïve, sweet outlook anymore. And while you gain grit, you still need to mourn what was lost along the way.

TIME DOES NOT (HEAL) AS MUCH AS AWARENESS DOES, AND THE "AWARENESS (OF) OUR CIRCUMSTANCES GETS US CLOSER TO HEALING THE AREAS WE'VE ABANDONED.

Signing divorce papers made me feel like I'd accepted my circumstances before I had a chance to mourn them. I didn't really allow myself to go through the grief cycle. What I thought was acceptance was really denial. Do you deny your feelings? Like, deny you should even have them?

Sometimes it takes our most painful experiences to acknowledge what mattered and what we ignored. Sometimes it is our circumstances that shape us into who we were meant to become. We may never have understood our significant value without the painful circumstances. Learn to understand the pain as a steppingstone toward healing. So when you say hello to your old self, tell them it's been a while but you'd like to have a conversation to go over everything, and this time the days that go by will only contribute to healing.

reflect

What areas of your younger self do you need to mourn? What losses are you scared to acknowledge? If you feel stumped, ask God to reveal to you some of the not-so-obvious things that may be keeping you from healing and growing. Use this section to help you identify and make a list of the heavy things you need to get off your chest.

This may present an opportunity to pray over the losses you are not acquainted with yet. Maybe loss of youth, beauty, home, crush, childhood dream, long-term goal, job, or money, or losses due to moving or betrayal.

Purpose

pur·pose | \'pər-pəs\
the reason for which something is done or created or
for which something exists

What is the purpose of all this? Will you find meaning in this pain?

Yes, of course, but here is the thing: you already had meaning before the pain. It is crazy to think about, but God had you in mind before you were born. Pain has purpose, but we had purpose before the pain.

I recall having lots of conversations with God when I was young. I grew up in a Christian household, but faith was never forced on me; it was something for me to freely walk into and explore.

Because of this openness and my atypical upbringing, I developed rose-colored glasses when it came to all the possibilities in life. I never felt I needed to live in a box or fit into a mold of what was considered normal.

When I was eleven, my parents broke the news that I would have to repeat fifth grade because of my poor grades. They anticipated that I would be discouraged, but I thought it was awesome because for the first time I thought I might be considered average sized and wouldn't get picked on and bullied for being small. Plus, I might finally be popular because I already knew all the test answers. Classic rose-colored glasses.

Neither wish came true. I was still the smallest by a foot, and I was still bullied. I still needed a tutor, and to top it off, I was diagnosed with ADD that year. But I kept trekking. Bravery is being terrified while remaining resilient. That was me.

Many years later, after working at my parents' thirty-five-year-old furniture company for a couple years, I began working for a global ministry called Orange. I suddenly found myself entering data into spreadsheets (no one should have trusted me with spreadsheets). I worked my way into other areas of the ministry, including helping with their leadership conferences. And after four years, I'd become one of Orange's art directors.

At dinner with the team one evening, the founder asked me what I thought was a trick question. He looked at me and said, "Eryn, the sky's the limit—what do you want to do? What are your aspirations?"

In the moment, I couldn't answer. I think sometimes we get so scared to admit our dreams or what we think our purpose is out of fear that someone will tell us we are unqualified. I remember later I was doing laundry and thinking, *Be honest, Eryn. What do you really want to do?*

Music . . . if I am honest. I want to pursue music.

I had prayed this prayer since I was in seventh grade: "Lord, let my voice be used for good. Let me have a light so bright that people ask where it came from." So, maybe that meant literally using my voice for good.

I called a music producer and told him I wanted to produce four songs. I didn't know which songs yet, but he believed in me enough to bring me into his studio with a writer. I spent nine hours in the studio with him and left with one song. Over the next couple years, all while working full-time at Orange, I released two albums and a few singles, licensed my songs to TV shows and commercials, and saw my music videos go viral. I thought maybe I had found my purpose.

As all this happened, a new desire slowly came over me: I wanted to create a product for the people who supported my music. But I couldn't afford to print T-shirts, so instead, I went to a craft store and picked up some cardboard stencils and fabric spray paint. I grabbed an old tee from my closet, and I decided to test out spray painting a few words on my own shirts. I started pretty simple with some basic phrases:

You Are Beautiful
Shine Bright

And then came a new phrase. I don't think it came from me—it felt more divinely inspired:

So Worth Loving

As soon as I saw it, I thought to myself, *That is so powerful, it has to already exist; someone has to own the trademark.* But no one did.

Spray painting was fun, but I wanted to connect on a deeper level with the people who believed in my music. I wanted to know their stories. Who were they? Why me? Why listen to my music? I wanted to encourage them. Most of all, I wanted them to know that their past mistakes didn't define who they could become. I wanted them to believe, despite whatever opinions were swirling around in their heads, that they were worthy to be used for good. And when I look back, I can say without a doubt, I desperately wanted to be told that as well.

So, I put my home address on my music blog and asked people to send me one of their shirts through the mail. I promised to spray paint "So Worth Loving" on each and every shirt. When I finished, I would mail back their shirts at no cost, with no fuss. For free. If they included some money for shipping, great, but if not, that was okay too!

I honestly thought I'd receive two shirts in the mail and that both would be from my mom. But I started receiving shirts from all over the country and the world. From North Carolina and

Hawaii—even from New Zealand. I remember receiving shirts that smelled like freshly cleaned laundry and thinking, *Eryn, don't mess up this shirt; it's her favorite, and you can't afford to buy a replacement.*

Eight months and hundreds of stories into my spray-painted-shirt project, I quit my job (against my accountant's advice) and dove into starting a T-shirt company.

My motivation was simple: I wanted to reach as many people as possible with this message, while keeping my new endeavor sustainable. How can I get a shirt into the hands of the girl who is struggling with self-harm or the guy who was sexually abused? How can I get a shirt to the woman who feels the shame of a divorce or to the kid whose heart has been shattered by a father who never said he was proud of him?

So Worth Loving. It isn't just a product. The products we now create are a bridge to meet people where they are, but the words are a lifestyle, a belief in how we view ourselves. A friend once said to me, "Maybe So Worth Loving isn't just a way for you to remind others, but perhaps it's your refuge, Eryn. Maybe you desired so badly for someone to tell you that you are worth loving that you started this movement and told others what you wish you could believe about yourself."

I think he was right.

I received stories from so many people who simply felt alone or ashamed, just like I did, or who were feeling the weight of yesterday, staggering through today, and hoping for a better tomorrow, just like I was. With their permission, I shared their stories on my blog.

There were times in my life when I just wanted to wake up and not feel anxiety in my chest or in my fingertips. I wanted to fully embrace that I was worthy of genuine, real, true love. That all the parts of me were worthy. Not the perfect parts, not the unmessy parts, but all the parts. And this community, this family—my family—all wanted to feel the same thing.

Fast-forward nine years, and after many wins and many mistakes, we've sold clothing to people in all fifty states and over thirty countries, we've operated a brick-and-mortar store, and we've seen lives change. What started as an idea and was birthed out of my water-heater closet turned office has now been able to tour the Southeast in a Sprinter van, visiting coffee shops and hosting small gatherings on over a hundred college campuses, all around our mission of helping people believe the truth that they are so worth loving. We've heard stories of our message preventing suicide and encouraging people to seek help. Through So Worth Loving, I've seen the true beauty of community, and I've seen safe spaces created for individuals to show up and be who they truly are, individuals who are willing to ask questions and who desire that grace be extended to them.

My desire to be known and loved made its way into my life's calling. Every day I get to think of ways to get the message into the hands of others that they, too, are worthy of love. While I may or may not operate So Worth Loving forever—maybe I still will when I am ninety-eight—I know that for the rest of my life, I hope to show up and remind my friends, on the dark days and on the ordinary days, that they are so worth loving.

Each of us desires to carry this message. Each of us desires for this way of thinking to be our place of refuge. Our purpose on this earth is to share that everyone is worth loving, and that purpose came before we even knew how to say those words. While pain can magnify our questions, God will walk us through healing the pain and we will see our purpose on this earth with a newfound lens. Better than rose-colored glasses. After seeing thousands of stories, I can confidently say that you had purpose before any hard season hit, and God will repurpose the pain from what was meant to break you down to gift someone else the reminder that they, too, are so worth loving.

Be ready to see your purpose in a new lens, and if you want to take a leap and your accountant tells you that you shouldn't, maybe that's a sign you should.

A gentle reminder:

> There is a story in your eyes. If you are tired, if you have feelings in
> this season of your life and you don't know where to place them, I
> hope these words will add peace to the chaos that may be swarming
> inside as you've begun identifying what you are carrying.

I wrote this in my journal on one of my darkest nights. I wanted
to remind myself of this. And I hope it helps you as much as it
did me.

Your eyes have seen things. There will be a day when those tired
eyes will share what you've seen. What mistakes you've made. What
mistakes you've seen others make. You will share what your heart
felt in those moments. You will share your imperfections. You will
share the aches and fears you feel. You will be able to share why
you were tired and drained. You will share what actions you chose
and what actions you did not. There will come a time when you
are healed from the pain and you will share because you've learned
to live in freedom.

You will share what your eyes have seen because, maybe, if it
helps one person, that means the pain wasn't pointless. You will
be able to share how focusing on thankfulness is the only path
forward—why you get out of bed. You'll share what being stripped
down meant to you while you're being built back up. You will tell
how you are able to see past the moment and understand a bigger
purpose in all of this. Maybe your eyes were heavy. Your heart was
heavier. But you are learning how to lay down that weight. You
know the capacity it takes to love yourself; perhaps you loaned
that capacity to other people thinking they'd do a better job. But
that's not possible for them. However, you will find out who can
love you, and that will allow you to feel peace for the first time.
You will share the discovery that the God who designed you will

have more grace, forgiveness, and adoration for you than anyone else. When you come back home to yourself, he will say, *I missed you*. No embrace can comfort the way his can. No voice sounds better than his does. He saw you at your lowest. His heart broke when yours did, and he knew how to piece it back together. He knew tape would only be a quick fix, so he broke out the glue.

The God who created you is continually gluing the pieces of your heart back together—no matter how many times he watches it shatter like glass against the wall. He has seen you trying to carry your brokenness alone, and he's saying, "This weight is too heavy for you, and the glass is too sharp to handle on your own. This will take a while, but you'll be fully alive again. Let me show you what kind of art I can create after it has been broken."

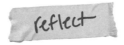

Below, pray specifically about what you want God to reveal as you identify what you are carrying. What are some things you want to give to God, and what are some things you aren't ready to relinquish just yet? It's okay if you aren't there! Acknowledging where you are and entering a conversation with God builds intimacy, and he desires to be close to you as you look in.

My prayers looked like this:

Lord, I don't know how to face this giant dark hole I am in. How do I identify what I am carrying? It all feels heavy: every decision I need to make and every choice I have made. Things that should be easy to do are hard, and the difficult things I'm dealing with feel like Mount Everest. How do I learn to trust you with all of this? What do you want? My phone bill? My doctor's bill? You see my finances and the stress. Is it weird to pray for money? Can I ask you to take my regret from last night? How do I surrender the friend who is not a positive influence but the only person who seems to be willing to show up for me in this season? Reveal to me what you want to carry and give me a peace that if you are real, you will carry it, and I can trust you. I'm new to this type of surrender . . . I just want some help. Will you help me? Amen.

Angry

an·gry | \'aŋ-grē\
feeling strongly that something is unjust or mean

Imagine a four-year-old girl with blonde ringlets, the youngest of three girls. She loves making mud pies and pulling onions from the fields. Her parents are from the Midwest but now live on sixteen acres of land in a small town of two thousand people in North Georgia, despite the fact that they don't speak a lick of Southern-ese. They're the creative type, who dreamed of living in New Mexico but settled for manufacturing Southwest-inspired furniture. They also collect school buses and old cop cars. They feed stray cats and breed Great Danes and Jack Russells (not together). They have an aviary of large red tropical birds called macaws, and at one point, they even had some wolves from Washington state, although if anyone asked, they were German shepherds.

Welcome to my wild upbringing. It was not at all your normal small-town southern-belle tale.

When I was little, there was a cat who made her home in the breezeway connecting our old country home to the guesthouse. When I was four, she gave birth to the cutest little kittens. And I *loved* kittens, so I spent lots of time admiring my new pals. During one of our play sessions, I locked myself in the breezeway while my mom and her friend were talking in the driveway. The breezeway had those old doors that would lock behind you when fully closed, and the only way out was to bang on the door until someone on the outside finally heard you.

So, picture me, this four-year-old little girl, straight-up panicking —banging on the door, hopelessly jumping up to see out the window that was about three feet above me. I was terrified that I had locked myself in there *forever*. Convinced my family would forget me and I would die in this little breezeway, I cried out for help as my little jaw shivered.

Haven't we all experienced a moment like that at some point in our lives?

All of a sudden, my mom saw my little body come bolting around the back of the house. I had sweat dripping off my ringlets and my face was beet-red from crying as I ran for my life and celebrated my freedom.

My mom looked at me with terror and concern. "Eryn! What happened, sweetie? Why are you running, and why have you been crying?"

"I got stuck, Mom," I told her. "I was playing with the kittens and got stuck, but then I prayed and now I'm not stuck anymore."

My mom looked at me, with extreme confusion on her face. "What did you pray?"

"I said, 'Jesus, you gots to help me.' And he did."

"What did he do?"

"He sent an angel."

At this point, my mom was so skeptical and confused. "What did the angel look like?" she asked carefully.

"Shirley Temple," I replied simply. "She got the door fixed."

Years later, my mom told me this story while we were sitting in a restaurant. I had just finished sharing my struggles with her. I was angry, jaded, tired, and confused. As I sat there, humbled, with devastation on my heart, my mom recounted this experience from my childhood. When she was through, she told the then-twenty-nine-year-old me, "That's when I knew you'd be okay in life. You knew who to ask for help at such a young age and from the bottom of your heart."

While it took me another year of pure stubbornness and some residual anger toward my circumstances before I admitted my situation was beyond my control, God loved me just the same as if I took that moment with my mom and applied that cry for help immediately.

Why do we resist talking to God and crying for help? What do we have to lose? Is it that we are scared he won't answer us the way we want? Is it that we struggle to believe God is real? Or is it that we are angry with him?

It was a gorgeous day. Spring was charging in. Birds were chirping and the sun was beaming in Georgia. I had just started to get my bearings, rebuilding my confidence and stepping back into the areas in my work that I was pretty good at. I had a new home, a new life, a new (old) last name. I was still me, but I was learning this new version of me. Prior to that season, I had decided to step away from So Worth Loving for almost two years as I took time to look inward. As I slowly took steps back into the company, I took on a new intern, and I decided to do a pop-up shop event. I was really excited. I felt a new wind. I felt like my old self in a new version, which just felt better. Stronger. Healthier. There were still weak moments as I was gaining back my strength; however, I hadn't felt this joy for retail in a long time. We arrived and the event couldn't have gone any better. Beautiful conversations were had, friendships begun, and product was sold. I left that night with the view of a sun-kissed sky on my way home. It felt as though God had painted it just for me, to affirm that I was where I was supposed to be. The next day as I unloaded my car, doing an inventory check, I noticed that our card reader was not properly connected to the iPad. I learned that we had given away more than half our inventory that evening. The transactions had never gone through.

My heart just sank, and I was thrown into a wave of inadequacy. Ill-prepared. Unqualified. Here, the waves of destructive words started to wash over me.

I was so done with the waves. I'd had enough of them. I felt like a crazy person. The waves of hopelessness would come in, tricking my mind into believing that happiness would never stay long enough for me to enjoy it. I'd be fine one day, but then it would take one thing done, said, or not said to trip the breaker and make the lights go out.

One of my friends, Kristen, caught word of our credit-card mishap. She had seen me try and try and try in my efforts to rebuild my life. She has a fund she pulls from when her friends experience a loss, and she gifted the company the amount we'd lost. The enemy had been using that situation to speak loud over me, and God used Kristen to be louder and help me recover quickly. God is just that sweet. He does things like this all the time when we turn our eyes to look for these moments.

The lights did not stop going out though. The waves of sadness, depression, and heartache just kept crashing in with every conversation I had with someone who wanted to know how I was, and also with the silence of old friends not asking how I was. Waves from mistakes of my own. From mistakes of others. I had to learn my triggers to control the waters.

After the waters settled, another big wave surfaced. Guilt of feeling happiness and guilt of enjoying God's faithfulness in slowly recovering and rebuilding my life.

There I was, tossed back into that tidal wave of another emotion to process. The waves kept me so inconsistent. In my commitments. My friendships. My work promises. I was so embarrassed by my lack of follow-through. I just continued to be tossed around by the new emotions I was not experienced in handling.

I was seeing a trauma therapist after the divorce. I had shared that I felt like I had no idea where I was swimming. I thought I was getting better only to find myself sucked back into the current of the aches in my heart. Why wasn't I getting better? I would find myself waking up and saying, "I think I will sleep all day."

My therapist said, "Eryn, depression can be an expression of suppressed anger."

That is exactly what I was doing: suppressing my anger. Not giving myself the permission to get angry. I used to be a hot-tempered little sucker, and over time when I felt my anger was dismissed in relationships, I stuffed it. I rationalized it. I said it didn't matter. I shouldn't be angry. I would say, *Well, Eryn, you did do* this *to deserve* that, or, *They didn't mean to,* all the while not allowing myself to be angry about anything. My spitfire mouth turned into a quiet one that invalidated my own feelings and rationalized someone else's behavior toward me.

I reframed my circumstances with an optimistic point of view, but it was actually a boiling pot of silent and suppressed resentment. My optimistic point of view was actually the denial of my anger.

So, with my therapist's recommendation, I made a list in my journal:

What am I angry at?
Well . . . I am angry at him for _____.
I am angry at her for _____.
I am angry at them for _____.
I am angry at me for _____.

I am *angry.*

When I said it out loud and when I journaled that list—valid, invalid, rational, or irrational—I recognized that I was angry, and I recognized the reasons why. For the first time, the first *real, honest* time, I saw underneath my anger. I saw the pain that had been weighing me down. I saw why the waves felt so heavy. I saw the triggers. I saw what had a stronghold on me. I saw what I could now articulate and ask for help with.

I learned that by expressing what I was angry about, I was also expressing what I cared about, what I had lost. Through my anger, I was expressing what I wished I could have done differently, what I wished others would have done differently.

Anger is such a powerful emotion. Anger shows you care. Anger reveals what matters to you. Anger reveals your boundaries. In certain circumstances, when I am upset with someone, it is more about how I allowed them to cross a boundary than their actually crossing it. Somewhere along the way, I lost my backbone for saying no and became a yes person, and I was angry at myself for doing that. I was angry at people around me for taking advantage of my yeses, and I was angry at myself for not having the boundary to say no.

Anger points to responsibility, and I had a lot to be responsible for. Anger is necessary for healing. When I admitted the anger I had suppressed, I also took responsibility for my part, and by doing that, I recognized what mattered to me and where the line needed to be drawn in the future.

So, if you are angry . . . good. It means you care, and caring shows that even after all you have been through, you can still vocalize what matters to you.

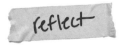

Here is your permission to be angry. So, what are you angry at? Who are you angry at? Fill in the blanks below to elaborate on why you are angry.

I am angry at him for _____.

I am angry at her for _____.

I am angry at them for _____.

I am angry at me for _____.

Lord, we pray that as we list the things that make us angry, you will affirm in us that it's okay to be angry. We know you will carry the anger for us. You will be gentle to our hearts as we reveal the things that have felt so heavy to admit. Lord, reveal in us what matters to us and what matters to you. I pray that you will help us process our anger and help us place it in a space where we can grow and develop strong boundaries that will protect our hearts. You are our Protector; teach us to trust that you will protect. Amen.

Drift

drift | \ˈdrift\
to gradually shift in position or be carried along by
the wind

If we allow ourselves to drift wherever we please, we will be an accumulation of whatever we pick up along the way. It takes consistent and continual discipline to focus on going in the direction that is good for us, and it also takes the courage to say no to the things that provide instant gratification.

When I became aware of the lens I had been living out of—the agreements, my appetite for instant gratification, the abandonment and people-pleasing I was prone to—it did not mean the work had been done. If old ways don't bring us down new roads, it's also true that we don't intentionally drift into healthy relationships and thriving careers. We don't suddenly quit abandoning ourselves and stop our desire for instant gratification. My awareness does not mean I will start to drift into the right direction. But don't you just wish sometimes that God could do all the hard work so you could live freely and lightly? In some ways, that "let go and let God" phrase is super appealing. I've often tried to make that phrase mean, *God, can you make self-discipline easier for me so this process doesn't have to be hard?* With no discipline, we will drift back into the same places. God has designed each of us to be so different from each other, but I think we all can agree that saying yes or no to some things will lead to either bettering ourselves or deteriorating ourselves. There are things we can do that will make the healing and the path forward a little easier on us. However, sometimes it's tough choices that will stop the drifting into old ways. These choices won't feel natural because they're not natural when your tendency has been toward poor choices and heartache.

The hard truth is that addictions don't suddenly manifest and codependency isn't suddenly formed. Bankruptcy does not just happen. Friends don't just walk all over you. There are many choices that we make out of our agreements that over time cause us to drift further and further away from who we desire to be and how we desire to love and be loved. One day, you'll wake up and ask, *Whoa, how did my life suddenly come to this?*

Drifting is a killer to dreams. It is a killer to relationships. To drift is to allow our craving for more and our unaddressed agreements to be the reckless drivers in our lives. Drifting is denying we have a choice to change our story. When we choose to be disciplined in stopping the drift, we choose to live with integrity. *Integrity* by definition is a belief in a code of values, honesty.

Let's be honest. What are your values? What is important to you?

When I'd considered those questions in the past, I can't say I ever really articulated an answer. I had journals of prayers, and I had documents I'd created in Google Drive that listed my company's values. But me? I guess I just assumed I knew what my values were. I think I assumed what they were based on my upbringing, and I counted on my ex-husband's values to help fill in the gaps where I was uncertain. I just kind of went with it. I guess you could say I drifted in and out of what felt right or good but never really defined what was important to me. If I am honest, I think I was scared to commit to any values, because what if I changed my mind?

During a hard season and in my desire for a new way of life, I started to look around at the people I admired. People I was inspired by. They could articulate so clearly what kind of person they wanted to become, and their life was a reflection of what they defined as important to them. Their life was a product of their many choices just like mine was, but my life was not a healthy product . . . it was an inconsistent one that needed a lot of attention and reevaluation. My life was a product of my beliefs.

Are your choices made out of your values or are they made out of your wounds? My present was shaped by my past, but I have a choice to shape my future. I can't go through life without being wounded, but I can choose to not live my life inside my wounds. There is an honest fight I have with my temptations. A fight in my daily life to believe that I am worth loving. God is not scared of this fight of mine. He watches me, ready and eager to be invited in. I know he wants to help me with my drift and redirect my steps, but I often think I'm strong enough to do all the work on my own. Other times, I get really tired and would rather God just do all of it without my lifting a finger, but I think a middle ground can be found. God wants to meet us exactly in the middle of these questions.

To choose to stop drifting takes so much attention and strength and *loads* of kindness toward yourself. It is hard. And if you are like me, you may feel embarrassed about your relapse into poor choices. I didn't know how to extend grace to myself; it took a minute before I knew it was a process and not a destination. The embarrassing part is slipping back into old ways once you've chosen what's healthy. You feel guilty. You feel like you just botched your whole path . . . and you start to notice that people will have strong opinions about it one way or another. Growth is not comfortable. Choices that are healthy for us are hard. It takes work. It takes courage. And listen, you will be rejected by some of your closest friends by choosing what is healthy for you. They are used to the old you, and if you choose to step into a new you with the belief that you are worth choosing, the true friends will stay and champion you. A healthy life is not a flawless life, but it is a reflection of how we view ourselves. It is the mirror looking back at who we are, how we treat ourselves, and how we encourage others to treat themselves.

In that continual battle to choose what is important to you, wisdom is birthed. It comes from the pain of changing course and being disciplined in healthy choices for yourself. But I will be real: sometimes I just have not known where I'm going. And choosing what is familiar seems safe, but familiar is not always healthy. In the past, I have not really trusted myself because of where I have landed before. Oftentimes, I feel like I am taking a guess in the dark. And when you have a relationship with the dark, that is the last place you want to return. It is easy to freeze and not make any decisions, and yet that is still making a choice.

When you integrate discipline, it will interrupt your drift. As you start to learn more about your values and more about the truth under the hurt, be flexible. Flexibility gives you grace when you slip up in being disciplined. Flexibility is a friend to discipline. Discipline is a process. If you mess up, it's not a reflection that you won't ever heal or get better. Knowing there is flexibility in your journey to be disciplined gives you the grace you need to begin building the muscles that will enable you to know what to say yes or no to and mean it enough to stand by it.

Some Things I Had to Ask Myself after Looking Inward

Are my choices a reflection of where I want to be, or are they a reflection of what I've always believed about myself (i.e., my insecurity, lies, distrust, lack of self-worth)?

A second question I had to ask myself was, *Are the people I surround myself with, the people who have a strong influence over my life, drifters or are they disciplined?*

Those were hard questions for me to answer because the answers revealed that my choices were not positively influencing my life. The people I had been surrounding myself with were okay with the choices I was making because, ultimately, they were making the same ones. They were drifting too.

Flexibility and Discipline Stop the Drift

Flexibility and discipline go hand in hand.

Do I like to work out? No, but when I do, I feel better.

Eat healthy? No, but when I do, I have more energy.

Wake up early? No, but when I do, I get more done in my day.

Take my makeup off? Not really, but when I wake up, I feel more refreshed.

Do laundry? Nope, but when I do, I have more clothes to wear.

Answer emails? No, but when I do, I value the sender of the email.

Pay bills? Nope, but when I do, I have electricity and water.

Saying yes to these things is good for me, my home, and my company. So, what are your lifestyle nonnegotiables? What characteristics will you look for in the people you surround yourself with, and how will you spend your time as you rebuild your life?

I've learned our choices in our friendships are a little bit more complex than a choice to pay our bills, but we still decide what we let in while we are learning what not to let in.

While no one can make me do anything, people can have influence over me, and during one of the most raw, impressionable times of my life, I definitely leaned toward what made me feel better versus what was healthy. So, if you need to create some distance from a friend who is influencing you poorly, that is not a reflection of your love for them but an act of discipline. No matter how sensitive I am toward friendships that need a little distance, feelings will be hurt. Discipline is uncomfortable, but being uncomfortable leads to growth. During my times of greatest struggle, I wanted a new path and healthy friendships. I wanted them badly!

So badly that being uncomfortable saying no to things over time started to feel like freedom. Any shame I had was now starting to break off. I felt more empowered because I started to see the fruit from saying no. I started seeing my self-esteem take shape, and I started exercising my newfound belief that I am worth loving. I am worthy of healthy choices.

We have already been accepted by God as is, and we want our choices to reflect that truth. I want that for you too.

Have I convinced you to stop the drift?

The truth is, I had a choice. I didn't have to keep drifting into unhealthy friendships and job opportunities out of a poor view of myself. I had to ask myself, *Will I be courageous enough to choose to change the course I've been drifting in?*

I came to the conclusion that it would not be a comfortable choice to make. Here are some ways to take control of the drift:

1. Identify your values.
2. Accept discomfort.
3. Make a list of nonnegotiables to stay grounded—say no to the things that cause drifting. Say yes to the things that contribute to healing.
4. Identify accountability partners and share everything with them—text two friends and ask them out for coffee, share the areas where accountability is needed, request confidentiality, and ask that they check in for continued accountability.
5. Be kind to yourself; celebrate small wins.
6. Repeat—you may have to repeat some of the steps over and over again, and that is normal and okay!

WE DO NOT DRIFT
INTO A HEALTHY
LIFESTYLE;

WE DISCIPLINE
OURSELVES
INTO ONE.

Discomfort

dis·com·fort | \dis-ˈkəm(p)-fərt\
a mental or physical uneasiness

Do you move past pain quickly? Throughout my life I've tried to move from the discomfort to comfort, even if it was temporary. I had the free will to make that choice and oftentimes, it was the one I made. However, that discomfort was not getting the honor it deserved. Growth hurts, and we should respect our discomfort enough to acknowledge it, but I often chose to avoid the pain.

When we're given the opportunity to face our discomfort and grow, we have two choices: denial or acceptance. Denial is refusal to admit the truth. When we live by the influence of denial, we live by our own strength and our appetite to appease our pain. Denial is far easier and less painful on the front end but more devastating to our hearts on the back end. Acceptance and ownership are more painful on the front end but less devastating to our hearts on the back end. What path will you choose?

"For the mouth speaks from the overflow of the heart," says Matthew 12:34 (CSB).

Have you admitted the condition of your heart? What is your heart full of? What have you denied? And what discourages you and makes you uncomfortable? What pain have you been fleeing from?

During my separation, I moved out of my house and stayed at my friends' place while they were out of the country for a few months. During that time, they forgot to pay the electricity bill. It was July, in the middle of the summer in the Georgia heat, and if you know what the Georgia heat is like, then you know what I'm talking about. It was around 110 degrees, with no exaggeration. During my stay, the electricity went out, and I couldn't get in touch with them to get it back on. The heat was horrendous. It was so uncomfortable, it affected my sleep. I didn't want to be there.

In all the discomfort of my circumstances and the surrounding conditions, there was a man who offered to let me stay at his place. Now, let's be honest, I knew that if I made the choice to stay at his place, it would not lead to anything good. It would temporarily feel good to be removed from the discomfort I was in, but the long-term choice would not be a good or an honorable decision. My desire to feel comfortable and needed was so sensitive and fresh that every form of my insecurity would come out if I chose to stay at his place that evening. I knew it would not honor my mind, my spirit, or my soul, but man, would the temporary relief of all the turmoil in my heart be silenced for a moment. While staying at his place would bring me a level of comfort, it would actually cause more discomfort over time. So, with temptation awaiting and temporary relief knocking, I called my mom. I told her, "Mom, this is just horrible. I can't sleep at night." And at that point, other things were going awry in my life, and the heat was just the icing on the cake. I'm sure you have at one point or another found yourself wondering, *Could just one more thing go wrong?* I told her, "Mom, I think I'm just going to go over to his place."

She said, "Listen. You will not go over to his place."

I said, "Mom, I'm so uncomfortable. This is terrible. I'm already displaced. I'm already not living at my house. I'm already in a separation. I'm already in debt. I'm already trying to do this and this and this . . ." I gave excuse after excuse to convince myself that this decision would not be *that* bad. I was on a rationalization ride.

We can be really clever in how we rationalize our entitlement for comfort, can't we? We can convince ourselves of anything without really trying, and in desperate times we can rationalize some really desperate choices. I've so often heard it said that desperate people do desperate things.

My mom said, "You are in this, Eryn, whether you like it or not, and making more poor choices will not help you out of this. Sometimes you gotta sit in the heat in order to know that you never want to be back in it again. If you can control it, you can control it."

If you can control it, you can control it. While there were a lot of things I could not control in that season of my life, saying no to the things that would lead me further down a path of destruction and denial was something I could control.

And it was in that moment that I decided I would not just stay, not just sit, but I would lie in the heat. I would start accepting and owning that this was where I was.

Devastation is a gift for us to become more aware of our denial. The longer we deny, the further the infection grows. The longer the infection stays, the further we get from healing, the further we get from where we really, truly, deep down in our core, want to be. We rarely respect someone who always says yes. Yet, we say yes a lot to be respected. What are you saying yes to for comfort when you might need to be saying no for the health of your body, your heart, your spirit? Who are some friends you might need to say no to? Or maybe even family members? What discomfort are you avoiding while the circumstance is getting worse?

Discomfort and discouragement show us what we believe in and how we see ourselves. They can actually be a wonderful gift. While they may not feel like a gift, they may show us the direction we should take. Discomfort shows us what we are uneasy about, and discouragement shows us the deprivation of our confidence. By having that knowledge, we then can start making different choices that will help us heal and get on a path that is healthy for our hearts.

Confronting discomfort makes me feel not okay, and I want to be okay. If you find yourself feeling that way, I will remind you of this: it is okay that things are not okay.

You'll question why people or places can leave such an imprint on your life. You'll be curious about what your purpose is, what the point is of what you are going through. You will wonder how all of this will shape you in the end, and you might be scared to discover who you are on the other side. You'll have thoughts about why you said yes to some things and turned away other things. You'll have moments of sheer victory and moments that will leave you brokenhearted. You'll experience emotional highs, and you will feel the barrel of the lowest lows. You'll learn what makes you feel alive, you'll learn what makes you cry, and you'll learn what makes you grow in a healthy direction. And in those moments, you may think maybe you just need a pep talk or words of encouragement . . . but I want to tell you this: let yourself feel and let yourself cry. Let yourself feel every ache and pain. Every ache and pain you denied out of shame or fear. Let yourself feel it. Let every drop come out of your eyes; don't hold it in. Let it out. Ask the questions you need to ask. Let your willingness to be vulnerable shape you and form an emotional depth you did not know you were capable of.

The life you live and every emotion that comes can be used to help another person you may cross paths with. Don't cheat yourself out of the opportunity to sit in your story, because one day, you will know how to be fully present for someone else. What you are experiencing may actually not be the end of something but the beginning of something, and in this moment, as you allow yourself to feel everything, you are learning to get to the other side.

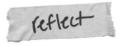

A prayer; an expression addressed to God . . .

God, I pray that when we look in, you speak up. I pray that when we look in and you speak up, you pour out your presence as we reflect. I pray that if we write our prayers in the margins of this book, those words will reveal how much you love us. I pray for protection over our thoughts. It takes bravery to acknowledge the things that we are carrying and the things that are within. Lord, I pray that we will have extreme grace for ourselves as we start to identify what is just too heavy for us. Lord, I pray that we will receive the grace you have for us and that when we write down the burdens we've held, with every pen stroke we'll be filled with a whisper of your love over what we are acknowledging. Lord, in Jeremiah 31:25 [CSB], it says that you "satisfy the thirsty person and feed all those who are weak." I pray that as we acknowledge our thirst for surrender, you feed us with your love and protection. It's in your name we believe you will do a work in us. Amen.

LOOK UP

---

understanding where your worth comes from

As I wrestled with what I discovered while looking in, I was skeptical about whether my desires would be accepted if I surrendered to God and lived with the belief that he is who he says he is. Would we be on the same page? Would he shoot down my ideas about where I wanted my life to go? Would he make me live a boring life? Maybe that sounds selfish to you, or maybe it resonates, but I wasn't convinced that God's desires for my life had any connection to my heart's desires. It seemed like we were on different teams.

Plus, when I looked in the mirror, I saw all the places where I felt inadequate and all the things I thought I was ill-equipped to handle. Because I saw them, I assumed God did, too, so why bother believing I could be used for anything worthwhile? I certainly didn't believe it, so why would he?

It wasn't until I began to recognize the lies I was telling myself and identify the unhealthy codependencies I'd developed that I was able to release control and say, "Okay . . . I'll look to you . . .

show me." And when I finally did, I discovered that it's less lonely and more fulfilling than trying to do things on my own.

When we begin to understand that God views us as infinitely worthy and acceptable, we can begin to view and accept ourselves that way too. And then we can fully live and embrace the life God desires for us.

And as it turns out, his desires for us actually vastly exceed ours. Our hopes and dreams are so small in comparison to the life he wants to reveal in us. For me, I had to explore all the other outlets and avenues before I could accept and believe that was true. I had to get to the end of myself before I could see there was a new beginning he had been working on for years.

After my divorce, my parents graciously let me move home to reset and rebuild my life. One night, I was sitting across the table from my dad as the three of us quietly indulged in another effortlessly beautiful and delicious meal from my incredible chef of a mother. In that seemingly peaceful moment, there was something I had to say, even though I knew it'd be the last thing my Christian parents would want to hear. But I just couldn't keep it in any longer, and I blurted out, "I'm angry at God."

At the time, I thought Christians didn't get divorced and they shouldn't be angry at God. And there I was checking off both boxes, so I wasn't sure what to expect in response. I heard my dad take a deep breath as he wrestled with how to respond. My mom's eyes were glued to him, and I could feel the tension between what she thought he was going to say and what she wanted to say first.

He said, "Eryn, don't be angry at God," which caused me to defensively snap, "Well, I am, so you can't just tell me not to be." Then my mom chimed in, "Sweetie, God loves you." To her disappointment, that didn't change the way I felt, and my dad and I continued to heatedly debate. I don't remember all of what was said, but I'll never forget how he ended it: "Eryn, you can be angry at God; just don't stay there."

If you find yourself angry . . . you can be . . . just don't stay there.

Looking back, I realize what my dad was feeling in that moment was heartbreak. Heartbreak that his thirty-year-old daughter was back home, divorced, and angry at God. He was feeling what my heavenly Father was feeling . . . heartbreak for how I was hurting, coupled with a desire for me to know how much he loves me.

I should have taken my dad's advice and tried to unpack why I was angry at God. But I didn't . . . I stayed there.

I remember, about a year later, getting home from the bar, feeling slightly intoxicated and more than slightly sad and empty. And not empty-stomach empty, emotionally empty.

Only five hours prior, I had been dancing around my bedroom to Camila Cabello's "Havana," applying makeup and picking out what to wear. Learning to embrace the single life again, I was headed out after a long week. Isn't that what you do? Get dolled up and go to dinner with your girlfriends? We were meeting at a beautiful restaurant in the city. The type where you walk in surrounded by leather, green velvet, marble side tables, and dark maple seats. And it's full of beautiful people too. Always dressed in the most current trends with their gold Rolexes, Tom Ford cologne, and perfectly coiffed hair.

I love my girlfriends and we had a wonderful evening. Starting off, we talked about life, work, what's new, and any dates we'd recently been on. And as usual, we ended up talking about what was stirring in our hearts. Our childhood wounds and attachment styles. Places where we still needed to heal and things we still wanted to do in our careers. We talked about the aches and pains that accompany our longing to love and be loved. The evening progressed . . . one drink, two drinks, more drinks bought by guys. Some innocent flirting and an Uber ride home.

After arriving back at home, I was greeted by my sweet French bulldog, Bernice (formerly known as Sprocket—after my divorce, I renamed her in honor of Bernice Pruitt from the movie *Hope*

Floats). I put my keys down, set my purse on the barstool, and stumbled into my bedroom in search of comfy clothes. I found myself staring at my reflection in the mirror, wrestling with the emptiness, trying to convince myself, *Eryn, what you are doing isn't as bad as how you feel about yourself.*

The bar wasn't bad. My outfit wasn't bad. The people weren't bad. My friends weren't bad . . . the only bad thing about this equation was the pain I had not surrendered, the anger I had not allowed myself to feel, and how those were causing me to view myself. I kept consuming alcohol and attention to fill the void.

I decided to put on a hydrating face mask and take a bubble bath. Surely, those would wash away the thoughts I had toward myself, the loneliness I felt, and the suppressed sadness I'd carried home from the bar.

As I floated in my tub, the water engulfing my body, only my face peeping out, I was thinking, *God . . . I'm so sad. I want to move forward, to pay my bills, to decide what to do with my company, to pick up the pieces of my life, but I feel so alone.*

In that moment, as all the thoughts started flooding my mind, I said out loud, "God, are you there? If you are really there, why have you not protected me? Why have you not stepped in? For years, I was in a relationship that made me feel like a crazy person. You saw that. You've seen all the injustice in my life. And you've seen my nasty sin that came from it. You've seen me in bed with a man who never had intentions to value me. You've seen the devastation an earthly love left me holding. You're supposed to be the one who can make all things right, but you've done nothing about it. I don't trust you. I feel abandoned. I feel alone. I feel angry."

I was angry at God and I still hadn't addressed why. Instead, I'd suppressed it and was now dealing with the emotional fallout.

Ultimately . . . my life felt like one big, *giant* mess, and I thought God was to blame. Not me. He was the reason I wanted to find belonging at the bar. It was his fault I sought attention from guys instead of from him. And since it was his fault, I decided to live my life my way and do as I pleased. With my newfound freedom, I began listening to podcasts and reading books that defied God. I was making a new life, and he had less and less of a place in it.

However, my new ways weren't paving a new road. Instead, I was going back down the same road, just with different outfits and a new hair color. Nothing about this new life made me feel more full or could replace the emptiness I still felt.

So, when I finally reached the bottom and asked God if he was there, it wasn't an entitled shout but more of a plea. "God, are you there? I grew up thinking you were, but that light inside me is growing dim. I'm getting more and more skeptical as I look around, and the Christians I see are scared to ask questions and seek the truth of who you are. I'm starting to wonder if I subscribed to this religion just because I was born into it."

Ironically, my wine consumption that evening didn't stop God from clearly answering my plea. Some of you might bristle at the idea of hearing God's voice, but I can't deny what I heard, and I can confidently say it wasn't my voice. Not only was his voice clear, the pressing of the Holy Spirit was so strong and beautiful. He said, "I know you have lived your way and it's been heavy for you. Would you trust and try my way?" In tears, I cried out, "You are right, Lord, and I will do whatever you want."

Just as you cannot patch an old garment with an unshrunk cloth, for the patch will pull away from the garment and make the tear worse, I knew my old ways wouldn't make a different path for me. I was that unshrunk cloth living out my old ways, making the tear far worse than before. I had a new life with a new last name, yet old ways of thinking. Both new and old brought me further and further away from God while tricking me into believing I was living my truth.

My spirit was so stubborn, jaded, and angry, and yet in one mere moment, I agreed to submit and began to fall in love with Jesus.

The Bible is *full* of stories of God bringing the broken back to life. It says he draws near to the brokenhearted.

The LORD is close to the brokenhearted and saves those who are crushed in spirit. (Ps. 34:18 NIV)

God is close. He was close to me the whole time . . . but he wasn't going to barge in. And he's not going to barge in for you either. You have to want it so badly. You have to be at the end of yourself to recognize that this new way of living is the beginning of finding yourself.

You have to be *so exhausted* by choosing your way to know there is a better way.

God is close. But it is on you to invite him in. Just know that it's going to take work on your part. He'll be right there encouraging you, and he'll never leave you, but don't expect to sit in a lounge chair in the sun while he deals with the things you said yes to . . . he won't, nor should he. God will provide you a shovel, but you have to do the digging.

It took me a hot minute to get over myself and invite God close. It took a friend who had observed my choices to be straight with me. After watching me struggle, cry, and deny the relief God wanted to give, my best friend, Jay, said, "Eryn, you got yourself here; it's going to be you who has to decide to get yourself out of it."

While deep down I knew God was with me and I wouldn't have to do it alone, I needed to recognize God was waiting for me to invite him into my story. He was in the room with me, ready to talk, but I had to start the conversation. God draws near to the brokenhearted, and in my case, he was ready to mend my broken heart. I needed to hold my heart out in my hands and ask him to hold it now. Learning to look up is part of the process of building trust with God. It's accepting and believing that he really is the most qualified and trustworthy companion to share your shame story. Your shame story might be a long list of all the things you've done wrong, and it may feel wild to believe that he could love you anyway. But looking up is trusting that if you bare all the

LOOKING UP (IS)
TRUSTING THAT IF YOU
BARE ALL THE MOMENTS,
YOU'RE NOT PROUD OF—

MOMENTS THAT WERE
DESTRUCTIVE, MOMENTS
THAT WEREN'T A
REFLECTION OF (WHO) YOU
WANT TO BE—

GOD WILL LOVE YOU
REGARDLESS.

moments you're not proud of—moments that were destructive to your self-esteem, moments that weren't a reflection of who you want to be—God will love you regardless. Essentially, looking up is imagining there is a deeper love to experience from the One who created you. It's learning to trust him with your life.

The day I surrendered and invited God to draw close, I prayed that he would remove the stains from my choices and from the pain someone else inflicted on me. I asked him to take away the sting of every betrayed friendship and eliminate the hurt of every lover I'd found myself in bed with. As I started to see the evidence of my transformation take hold in my life, I learned more and more that God loves recovery. He loves redemption stories, and I wanted him to go crazy in my story. I recovered my life so much, and there is no denying he was by my side for all of it!

So, as we dig into this process of looking up, I encourage you to look to God. When I did, he drew near to me and recovered my jaded, broken heart. And I know he will do the same for you. He is just that loving. And you are just that worthy of love.

Each chapter of the "Look Up" section concludes with a breath prayer:

Breath: a pause in an activity

Prayer: an expression addressed to God

Breath prayer: a pause to express a moment or request to God

To me, a breath prayer is what you cling to throughout the day, something you say over and over to combat a thought or turn to God as you're trying to surrender and build intimacy with him. The words can be expressed as you inhale and exhale.

Intimacy

in·ti·ma·cy | \ˈin-tə-mə-sē\
something of a personal or private nature; nearness,
closeness

We all desire intimacy. We all want closeness. We all want to be near something or someone that makes us feel seen, loved, known, and heard. As people, our ultimate source of intimacy is found in our Creator. But too often we try to plug the holes in our heart with other things that make us feel temporarily seen, loved, known, and heard.

We are always just degrees away from building intimacy with God. He's always near and he's always willing, but many of us tell ourselves that he doesn't care or want to know us. I told myself there are bigger and worse cases than mine for him to tend to in this world. So, instead of bothering him with my stuff, I went on a search for someone else who cared to know me and wanted to know me.

I attempted to plug the holes in my heart with relationship after relationship. It worked for a little while, but it wasn't real intimacy. And the truth is, I was tired of it.

Are you as tired as I was? Are you jaded and worn out? Have you made decisions you thought would help you gain intimacy and remedy your pain but ended up making things worse, like I did? Well, I hope this is good news for the ones about to throw in the towel . . . God does not toss us away if we aren't perfect. We don't need to arrive at a certain point to be loved by him. He will lean in when we are willing to let him in. God wants to show us we don't have to be perfect to be seen and known. Our broken circumstances are used to create a level of empathy in us that more people need to encounter.

One person who helped me see that was my friend Joe. He has witnessed my entire journey, from the unraveling to the restoration. At each step, he encouraged me in a healthy direction while accepting where I was. Conversations with Joe always ended with "I love you. I believe in you."

One day, Joe called me and asked if I was dating anyone and I said yes.

"Well, who is it?" Joe asked.

I replied, "Jesus." I could hear Joe's eyes roll over the phone.

"Eryn . . . no thirty-two-year-old says they are dating Jesus; that's what you say when you're twenty-two years old."

"Well, Joe, I was married at twenty-two, and that didn't work out, so I'm trying it now."

We both laughed because it seemed funny, but it was exactly what I needed.

For a long time, friends had told me I should take a break from dating. That I needed to learn to love "just me." But I rolled my eyes at their advice and avoided all the books that encouraged taking a break from dating. I thought they were cheesy or insignificant, but the truth is, they were right. Dating without a break led me nowhere but to more heartache. I needed a change, so I decided to try it—I decided to take a year off from dating.

For the first few months, I had to completely detox my lifestyle: I avoided places that caused me to long for attention. Instead of filling my time in a bar, I'd fill it in a book. I grilled out with my neighbors. I focused on working out, going for long walks, and visiting my family more. I wanted to learn to be content with just me. But it was hard. Maybe you can relate. How many of us can confidently and consistently be content without using outside remedies to get a fix for validation or acceptance? I know it was a struggle for me.

Ultimately, I had to gather all my crap and all my mess into my hands, hold out my arms, and say, "God, if you are who you say you are, that means you want all of this." And, amazingly, what I came to find out is that he does. He wants it all. In fact, he yearns for that level of intimacy.

But how do we invite God into our circumstances? It's not something you can force. Intimacy is not about control but surrender. It's about revealing. Intimacy is revealing who you are and being loved more for it, all of it.

God's not interested in whether or not we can put on a perfect performance. He knows we can't. What he cares about is that we get to a place of acceptance and trust. He wants us to accept that he has the best intentions for our lives, accept that he has chosen to love us no matter what, and continue to develop more trust in him.

I struggle every day to accept that the Creator of the universe genuinely cares for me and that I do not need to perform for his love, but I can come to him with my heart, my soul, my mind—everything that makes up who I am—and he loves me the same.

It is really hard for me to fathom and trust that Jesus chose to wear the weight of my sin and say I am clean, even when I have done unclean things. But that's exactly what he did, and it's what he is trying to tell you and me right now, in this moment. He's whispering in the most compassionate, tender, guilt-free voice, "Look at me, as I hang upon this cross. This is for you. No other person will love you as passionately and intimately as I."

If I had to guess, you probably wonder the same thing: *Does God love me just as much when I'm self-centered or ridden with jealousy as he does when I'm self-controlled, making wise choices, and forgiving others?*

Yes, he loves us the same!

Imagine a relationship where you share your past, your family's history, your career hopes and future dreams, and you are met with only acceptance and love constantly for the rest of your life. No ego, insecurity, or expectation for you to perform a certain way.

That is what's offered here.

I don't know about you, but if it's true that God wants my heart, if he's really asking me, "Will you bring me in and allow me to romance you into a love you will never find on earth?" then I want to learn to dance with him minute by minute. Not just when things are bad. Not just when things are good. All the time. From the bottom of my heart.

I want to be immersed in understanding how God thinks of me. I want to discover how to consistently live my life out of his truth. A pure truth. An uncontaminated truth. That I am so worth loving. I want so badly to discover how to live in his thoughts and not my thoughts.

And while it sounds like a noble desire, it didn't and still doesn't come easy. I have to fight for it. I fight daily from the belly of emptiness. From the holes inside my heart. I fight to get out of my way and have a thirst for God.

And even still, sometimes I don't feel like reaching out to him. Does that ever happen to you? When you just don't feel it, you don't feel him? In those moments, we have to be honest. It's okay to let him know we don't feel it. I've had to recognize that I had an addiction to my feelings: too often I think that feeling something makes it true. I make the mistake of assuming that if I don't feel him, then he isn't there. My friend and mentor helped me understand why that isn't true. She assured me God is always there, and while my feelings are not invalid, they don't always present the whole picture. Just my perception of it.

This has really come alive for me since I've started waking up every morning and spending intentional time with God before tackling the onslaught of emails and text messages. I make coffee, listen to worship music, and invite him to share with me. Whatever he wants to share.

I tuck my phone away in another room, and I start off by praying, "Jesus, I invite you into this. I want to learn to hear your voice. I ask you to astound me and make it so clear when you speak that I cannot deny it."

And then I grab my computer, open up my notes, expand to full screen, and journal through the following questions:

1. What am I feeling? How are my mind, body, and heart?
2. What happened yesterday?
3. What do I feel heavy about? Do I feel guilty about anything? Surrender it.
4. God, do you have anything you want to say to me? What do you think?

Simply reflecting on my days, on my mind, body, and heart, has helped me so much. It's helped me learn the voice of God. And it's helped me recognize that he was already showing up way more than I ever realized, in the little areas of my life that I never gave him credit for. It's helped me understand the difference between feeling convicted and condemning myself. To convict is to acknowledge an act, and to condemn is to belittle, attack, and excommunicate.

It is so important that you read that again. God is not a condemning God. He does not belittle you—that voice is not his. So, when you decide to invite him in and embrace his nearness, know that he wants you to acknowledge destructive behavior from your past and present, but he is not going to belittle you for bringing it to him. Ever. The more you express your reality, the more you learn to be aware of your behavior and the more you learn his guilt-free, kind, and loving voice.

Living this out takes practice. My ways of learning to talk with God and listen for him might not be your ways. You have to find what works for you. Maybe it's nature walks or slow mornings. Whatever it is, prioritize intimacy with God as a daily routine and see what happens.

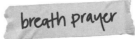

Lord, I want to know what intimacy means. True, real, honest intimacy. I pray that when my heart seeks outside validation, you will confirm in me the validation that no one can give but you. Confirm that I am loved, seen, known, and heard by you. Amen.

Endurance

en·dur·ance | \in-ˈdu̇r-ən(t)s, -ˈdyu̇r-, en-\
the ability to withstand hardship and stress

My parents had a furniture business. They sold their furniture in their retail stores and to other retail stores, and they would made beautiful fixtures for people's homes. Beds, dressers, armoires, coffee tables, chairs, benches, hutches—I mean, you name it, they would make it. Sometimes to keep a promise to a customer my dad would work late nights, and I would hang out with him when he did. My nine-year-old little self would make snow angels out of the sawdust, and I would ride my bicycle all over the factory. This furniture company was my parents' baby, and it was my playground. But there was one night we all will never forget. It is a memory that has left an imprint on our minds. It was a nightmare that we could not wake up from. That particular night, my mom picked me up for dinner. My dad shortly followed. We had just ordered food when a phone call disrupted our dinner. I remember my mom answering the phone and responding in a panicked voice, yet trying to get the facts before she broke down: "What's on fire? I need you to slow down. Our place? Which place? Our home? I don't understand what you are saying is on fire."

My parents' ten-year-old factory was on fire.

As we packed up our food and rushed over to the factory, we pulled up to find cars, fire trucks, and ambulances. But worst of all, my parents' dream—their baby, my playground—was burning in front of our eyes. The factory was filled with wood and lacquer and as lightning struck from the sky, it brought the building down to the ground in an instant.

In one moment, years of hard work turned into questions like "Are we going to start from scratch again?" "Can we rebuild this?" "Do we have the energy?" "The resources?" "Do we have a choice?"

My parents had no tools and no equipment, but they did have a small amount of money, a pocketful of belief in their product, and employees who believed in them. Their answers to all those questions? Yes, and they produced furniture for twenty-eight more years.

See, they had an outlook that caused them to bounce back from this extremely crushing circumstance. They had belief in themselves and in their product. Their belief allowed them to endure the pain and grow from it. They expanded their business all over the world and benefited financially from it. The second time around, they could endure the punches the small-business world offers and not flinch as they may have the first time. Their capacity for hardship became deeper, and their character was sharpened.

That is what God can do in the most crushing moments. Even when our life goes up in flames. We can rebuild better than before if we believe we can and if we believe he is right by our side when we get to work.

When things got hard, when things felt crushing, when I had no resources or financial aid, my parents' circumstance taught me to ask, *Well, Eryn, what do you believe? Do you believe you are worthy of the life you desire? Can you endure the pain you'll experience as you work through the muck, and do you believe this will sharpen you? Do you have a choice?*

Sometimes we can predict to some extent what the future may look like, but sometimes we have no idea if the discomfort we will experience is worth leaning into during rebuilding. Our circumstances can knock us down, but the belief in ourselves is what gets us back up. While our circumstances change, may our belief in our worthiness to rebuild and recover not waver.

I used to think being in a position of rebuilding was a consequence of mistakes, and while that can be true (and for me it was), I also think rebuilding might actually reveal what was buried in your heart to create all along. When we endure, we see what we are made of, what we desire more of, and what is of value to us. Endurance is our friend in rebuilding, and the tolerance we acquire to hardship shows us we can help others when they don't believe they are worthy of rebuilding. Your endurance can help someone else endure. What a gift. What a gift to offer another person: from the depths of your pain, you will be present in someone else's story. That is a belief worth holding on to.

> Consider it a sheer gift, friends, when tests and challenges come at you from all sides. You know that under pressure, your faith-life is forced into the open and shows its true colors. So don't try to get out of anything prematurely. Let it do its work so you become mature and well-developed, not deficient in any way.
>
> If you don't know what you're doing, pray to the Father. He loves to help. You'll get his help, and won't be condescended to when you ask for it. Ask boldly, believingly, without a second thought. People who "worry their prayers" are like wind-whipped waves. Don't think you're going to get anything from the Master that way, adrift at sea, keeping all your options open.
>
> When down-and-outers get a break, cheer! And when the arrogant rich are brought down to size, cheer! Prosperity is as short-lived as a wildflower, so don't ever count on it. You know that as soon as the sun rises, pouring down its scorching heat, the flower withers. Its petals wilt and, before you know it, that beautiful face is a barren stem. Well, that's a picture of the "prosperous life." At the very moment everyone is looking on in admiration, it fades away to nothing.

Anyone who meets a testing challenge head-on and manages to stick it out is mighty fortunate. For such persons loyally in love with God, the reward is life and more life. (James 1:2–12)

breath prayer

Lord, reveal to me what is true. Give me the strength to press forward when I feel I can't keep going. Give me the discernment when I am not sure what direction to take. Only with you, Lord, can I rebuild my life in a way that is sustainable and a true representation of your grace, healing, and mercy. Have your way. Amen.

Recovering

re·cov·er·ing | \ri-ˈkə-və-riŋ, -ˈkəv-riŋ\
being in the process of overcoming a shortcoming or problem

In Matthew 11:28, Jesus says, "Come to me. Get away with me and you'll recover your life."

Reading those words gives me so much relief and hope. "And you'll recover your life." Not maybe . . . but you *will*.

Recovering your life is an ongoing process. There are temptations that will creep in and try to hinder you from living out your healthy desires for yourself. But it is so important to be patient with yourself as you step into the process. As you do this, you will see how old ways of living bring a slow deterioration and an unsatisfied life. So, you adjust your lifestyle, try to get a hold on your temptations, learn how to not fall back into them, wrestle with the shame, give yourself grace, and keep moving forward. It's a cycle that you will find yourself in, and the more closely you pay attention, the more guardrails you will be able to put into place to stop the cycle from perpetuating.

If you grew up in or around church, you may have heard this process referred to as sanctification, which means to be made free from sin. To be set apart for sacred duty or use.

I think most of us have a desire to be set apart and used for something big. By *big*, I don't mean lavishly successful but simply able to learn more about who we are and how we were made so we can bring light and life to others. That could mean being an incredible, solid friend. Or being the most dependable employee. It's whatever you feel is God's purpose for you. That's what makes it sacred. God has gifted you with the ability to love and serve others in a unique way. By stepping into that awareness and living it out, you are constantly being refined as you learn to live freely, despite your past.

The first step to recovering is uncovering the unhealthy habits you don't want in your life anymore. An addict doesn't choose to be an addict . . . they choose habits that over time become their only source of relief. Whatever you water will sprout. Whatever you feed will grow. So, as you begin this process, you have to ask yourself, *What unhealthy habits am I watering? What harmful tendencies am I feeding?*

And then you can continue the recovering process by inviting God into your dark places, and with his help, learning to live in his grace. Ephesians 5 contains a few of my favorite verses on this.

For you were once darkness, but now you are light in the Lord. (v. 8 CSB)

Have nothing to do with the fruitless deeds of darkness, *but rather expose them.* (v. 11 NIV, emphasis added)

But everything exposed by the light becomes visible—and everything that is illuminated becomes a light. This is why it is said:

"Wake up, sleeper,
   rise from the dead,
   and Christ will shine on you." (vv. 13–14 NIV)

For too long, that was me; I was asleep. My fears and struggles felt like a weight stuck to my chest. One of my fears was that I was unlovable and would never be worthy of love. On my own, it was just a matter of time until I proved that fear right. But when

I invited God into my dark places, when I said, "God, here it is—here are all the things you see but I'm too scared or too prideful to tell you about . . . ," it was like the weight was finally lifted off my chest. Vocalizing my fear to God had a wild effect on my heart. That was when I began recovering and living a life free from my past mistakes. For the first time, I felt completely clean before I even attempted to do a thing.

Let's pause and sit in that for a minute . . . just bringing my fears and worries and struggles and temptations to light revealed the power of God's love for me. I didn't have to *do* anything. His love is not conditional. And while it was scary to confess the things that felt icky, when I did, I learned that he loves me more than I ever understood. Sharing with him only magnified that love to its true size and dissipated the fear. If you haven't experienced that, you can. You will. I can't tell you how amazing and awe-inspiring it is to receive love with no strings attached, with no performance required. All of me is loved just as I am. My search for love has ended. I will keep seeking God and, yes, I will fight my temptations and old ways because they don't die easily, but I am still loved in spite of them.

As we continue to uncover more of who we are, we also become aware of what we are not, and we learn to accept what we have done. This awakening can take us down one of two paths: a path of shame or a path of love. Rejection never has the final say, but it sure tries to. Instead, we have to learn to live with the deep assurance that we are fully loved. This posture of living loved is rooted in the One who created us.

Learning how to love ourselves is a journey to learning more about the source of love: Abba, Father, God, Holy Spirit.

As we learn more about him, we learn more about all the amazing things he has in store for us. But even as we rebuild and recover, we may find it hard to receive his blessings.

One evening, my friend Dee Dee and I were sitting by a fire discussing our relationships with God. I was asking her how, after all the mistakes I've made, I can still receive any blessings God would want to bring my way.

Dee Dee compared it to her relationship with her three-year-old little girl. She said, "If my daughter Lennie ever did something harmful to herself, of course my heart would hurt too . . . and if she came to me with it, I would grieve with her, but I would also love her in it. It wouldn't stop me from pursuing a relationship with her, and it wouldn't stop me from wanting to celebrate her. I couldn't imagine if ten months went by and I tried to encourage her and bless her with a gift or a birthday party, or a little treat, and she reminded me of that mistake she made ten months ago. I would be so heartbroken if she couldn't believe that I genuinely don't see her for the mistake she made. I would be so heartbroken if she lived more in her mistake than in the love I have for her."

The same is true with God. When we mess up, it breaks his heart. But what breaks it even more is when we deny his mercy, forgiveness, and grace. By doing so, we keep ourselves in a cycle of punishment and shame. And we stunt our ability to see and receive the gifts he has for us. Living in the process of recovering is continually reminding ourselves of the way he sees us. As beautiful and worthy.

What are some gifts you have felt ashamed to receive? Perhaps a healthy relationship? Or a bonus at your job? Maybe a fresh start in a new home?

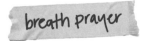

Lord, I pray I will see myself the way you see me, and I pray I may accept the gifts you are blessing me with. I pray that you will dissipate my shame and that I may hear only your voice of love and acceptance for who I am. Amen.

Sabotage

sab·o·tage | \ˈsa-bə-ˌtäzh\
deliberate destruction

We all have a little saboteur in us.

That's why we choose the foods we shouldn't eat, the people we shouldn't date, the jobs that don't value our worth, and the friendships that make us walk on eggshells.

I remember dating a guy who traveled a lot. If you have ever been in a long-distance relationship, you know that good communication is the only way to stay connected until you see each other again. This particular relationship ended after he ghosted me on one of our regular FaceTime dates. Afterward, I found pictures and video of him with two women at a club. When I confronted him, he told me that as he ignored my "Hey, are we still on?" text, he put on his boots to go out and thought to himself, *Am I sabotaging this relationship?*

Ouch. Right? *Geez, dude. What do you think? Maybe?*

While that experience left me feeling disposable and icky about myself, I've done similar things to others. I bet we all have in one relationship or another. Instead of walking toward conversation and sharing our struggles, we do the opposite. Out of fear, we flee from confrontation or pretend there isn't a problem. Really, we just don't want to reveal more of ourselves.

We sabotage because it's an easy escape route from intimacy. Intimacy is closeness. It is being seen for all of who we are, not just the pretty parts. That is in our inherent nature. It is how we are made. We are wired to be close, and we desire to be known and loved.

We sabotage because we feel something in us that we don't want to accept or acknowledge. And we don't just sabotage relationships with people; we do it with God too. Out of fear of being seen in the midst of our struggles, we choose not to show up and do our part in the relationship he has designed for us.

If that resonates with you, know you are not alone. I have pursued things that distracted me long enough to feel good, and when that wore off, I'd find myself doing it again. I've filled my wineglass too many times in order to avoid sitting in the presence of the Lord. I've sparked up conversations with people I am not interested in truly getting to know only to get something from them. These conversations allowed my insecurities to temporarily subside so I didn't have to deal with the wrestling in my soul.

Sure, in the moment, sometimes destruction satisfies a carnal desire, but rarely has it ever made me feel better. It almost always makes me feel worse. And leads to shame.

My fear of truly seeing myself or allowing God to see me led to hiding amid feelings of hopelessness, which led to the destruction and shame. I sabotaged. I would feel guilty and then distance myself from God because of shame and a disbelief that he could love me even after my eight thousandth mess up. After I was tired of it all, I shared my struggles with a friend, which led me to surrender to God and begin to forgive myself. I finally developed accountability and started becoming stronger. Looking back, I wish I had carried more softness and grace for myself as I was learning how to accept God's love. I know his heart broke to see how hard I was on myself in the process.

Being in debt had a huge impact on how I viewed myself. I had debt collectors calling me and I had bills due, but I didn't have the money. I was living off $800 a month and barely getting by. I remember one particular day that was an all-time struggle. Every bill I could think of shouted "Good morning" at me before I even got out of bed. My heart began pounding, and the anxiety started building. My thoughts quickly jumped from *How am I going to pay these bills?* to *God, do I have a purpose in life?* Boy, the pendulum swing is so extreme sometimes.

I wrestled with the patter of my fast-beating heart all morning . . . nothing could make it calm down. The truth was, I had so much fear built up that I hadn't shared with God. Things like doubt and unbelief. If I was honest . . . I needed to ask him the question that was lodged deep down past my pounding heart, the question I had been avoiding: *God, if I seek you with all my heart, give you all my fears, give you all the hard stuff, what's the trade-off? Will you actually help me? And if you don't, does that mean you don't love me?*

Have you ever felt skeptical that God will show up if you express all the problems you're experiencing? Or when he's not moving as quickly as you'd like, have you ever taken back all the things you surrendered to him and said, "Just kidding"? I know I have. I've tried to negotiate, and I've tried to give him my struggles but with conditions. "I'll trust you with this if the outcome is that." But let's be honest, ya'll; is that surrender? Is that true intimacy? Or is that a fear-driven relationship or an attempt to maintain control?

In that moment, I knew I could ignore my finances and allow sabotage to set in and destruction to pile up. Or I could give the destruction I'd created to that point to God and begin to trust that he would help me face the consequences of my actions and that I would learn something about myself in the process.

Because, ultimately, after all the metrics we find worth in are set aside or stripped away, the question we have to ask ourselves is this: Are we okay with what we see, and are we able to trust God on this journey? If not, we will continue to sabotage and choose destructive behavior to avoid facing the things we feel.

What are some areas in your life that you might be sabotaging?

Are you sabotaging a relationship, your finances, your career, your friendship with that person who keeps showing up?

Now I want to gently ask, What is that thing you are scared to bring to God that is potentially sabotaging intimacy with him?

breath prayer

Lord, let my soul and my spirit be strengthened by the adversity I face in this life. May you be the only One who can satisfy my need for security. May I trust that you are holding me up with every step I take out on the water. You will not let me sink. You will draw near and know my heart is fully surrendered to what you want. My old way is done, and the new way is yours. Amen.

Vulnerable

vul·ner·a·ble | \ˈvəl-n(ə-)rə-bəl, ˈvəl-nər-bəl\
capable of being wounded; to be fully yourself and
open to injury

Being vulnerable is allowing yourself to be open and honest, even though there is a risk of getting hurt.

Transparency is different. It's about being seen. We often hear someone say, "Let me be fully transparent," followed by their honest opinion, but it doesn't always come with an openness to being spoken into. Transparency can be like speaking with a wall up.

Transparency teeters on wondering if you're safe with walls up, while vulnerability is believing you're safe and letting the walls down.

Social media makes it easy to deceive ourselves and others about our level of vulnerability. We may come across as open and welcoming on social media by sharing the inner workings of our lives, but what we're really doing is controlling how our lives are seen while keeping our walls up against rejection and criticism. That's why many of us shape our lives to the tune of likes and comments. We want to be transparent but aren't willing to be vulnerable.

In the spring of 2017, I was in the midst of my separation. My life on social media looked a lot different from reality. I was consumed with making my life look better than it was in order to remedy the pain I was in. Beautiful filters, nicely shot photos of my home, naturally lit selfies, the works. From the outside, it looked like I had it all together . . . but I didn't. The more validation I gained for this portrayal of my life, the more I wanted my real life to reflect it. So much so that I started to deceive myself. I started to believe that those in the real world were wrong and everyone in my social media bubble was right. I denied what was true.

I wasn't open for feedback or criticism. I didn't want to be vulnerable. I only wanted to share my life and be the recipient of the applause that provided temporary relief.

What this taught me was that I had an intimacy deficit within myself and an intimacy deficit with God. We can't fully be in tune with the workings of our hearts without the willingness and vulnerability to open ourselves up to our God and listen. He has feedback, and it's probably not what you're telling yourself it is. It's not the same thing some judgy churchgoers have to say. The one who made us knows us best and knows exactly how to talk to us when our hearts are hurting. Remember, he draws near to the brokenhearted. He doesn't hurt the brokenhearted.

While I was stuck in denial, there was a lot of gossip swirling around me. A lot of judgment. A lot of hearsay. A lot of other Christians tearing down my beautifully captured life. I'm sure many of you have experienced that too. Regardless of whether or not some of it was true, I know God doesn't want his kiddos talking that way about each other. And he definitely doesn't want us believing that what others say about us is what he thinks of us.

And I know that he very clearly defends in Scripture those who are straightforward and honest. He defends those who suffer injustice and claims victory for them.

> In place of your shame, you will have a double portion;
> in place of disgrace, they will rejoice over their share. . . .
> For I the LORD *love* justice;

I hate robbery and injustice.
(Isa. 61:7–8 CSB, emphasis added)

He is so loving and so caring even when we are honest with what we've done and with the way we feel. He just loves that we are talking to him. He is close because he craves that connection, that vulnerability. When we are ready, he is there waiting. He has things to say and things to work out in us.

If you're like me, maybe you've had your vulnerability used against you. And so, for a long time you figured, why wouldn't God be any different? Well, I have good news for the tired heart. God's response will always come out of love, not out of condemnation. His response to your honesty won't be the same as that of anybody who may have hurt you. His response every time is going to be, "Hey, you, I love you. You're awesome. Let's go do something together."

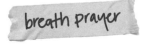

Lord, I know that inexperience is not a sin. I pray that, through my bravery to step out and be vulnerable, you will teach me more of what I am capable of. I pray for protection over my mind and body as I learn to be more vulnerable with you and the safe people in my life. Give me strength to trust again. Amen.

Lies

lies | \\'līz\\
fabrications, distortions, misinformation

Can you remember a time in your life when you found yourself looking in the mirror wondering how you got to that point? A time when you were making decisions that negatively impacted your heart and your body?

Me too. I have said yes to more things than I've said no to. I have agreed to things that only minimized my worth instead of reflecting my significance. I have made bad decisions because it's what I thought I deserved.

After coming to the end of myself, being so tired of continuing to feel discouraged, unloved, and extremely insecure, I knew I needed to make a change.

What I discovered was that the common thread in every decision I was making was the long list of lies I believed about myself. Many were subtle or even seemed like normal things to believe based on society's standards.

These lies weaseled their way into my life, and I mistook them for truth. They became my mask, and I allowed them to make decisions for me.

And the lie at the core of it all was that I was unlovable. I believed that if I was more of X or less of X, then I would be lovable. *If only I could look a little more like this or behave a little more like that* . . . My lies developed into an equation, and I thought if I could become the answer to the equation, then everything would be okay.

Lies are so sneaky and deceiving. There are even a million meanings of the word *lie*. It can mean to speak falsely or utter untruth. Or to hoodwink, misinform, or mislead. Probably the most familiar definition is an untrue statement made with the intent to distort.

You may have heard this quote, commonly attributed to Gandhi: "Your beliefs become your thoughts, your thoughts become your words, your words become your actions, your actions become your habits." I'll add my own ending and say your habits become your lifestyle.

What I believed about myself had manifested in my actions and developed into a lifestyle. And it was all based on lies! Because I felt unlovable, I sought out guys and status to feel loved and seen.

To be seen as having value, I thought, *I need to be smarter. I need more money. If I date a guy people respect, then people will respect me. If I had clothes like this. A home like that. If I was more fit. If my makeup brand was this. If my shampoo was that. If only I was friends with so and so.*

Does any of this sound familiar? It's sneaky, huh? Money is not bad. Intellect is good. A guy people respect is a representation of his character. Dressing well shows you honor your body. However, I was placing my value in these things. In fact, I thought if these things weren't part of my equation, then I had no value.

And because I thought of myself this way, my lifestyle and my relationships were a product of these false truths.

First Corinthians 13:4–5 (NIV) says,

> Love is patient, love is kind. It does not envy, it does not boast, it is not proud. It does not dishonor others, it is not self-seeking, it is not easily angered, it keeps no record of wrongs.

When I looked at my life, I realized I was not talking to or treating myself with love. I was talking to myself with conditions and absolutes. Quite the opposite of love. Any love I had toward myself was conditional and performance driven. What I needed to do was still myself long enough to quiet my voice and listen for God's.

Where I live is basically Narnia. Just kidding. I wish! But it is a beautiful little nature oasis with waterfalls and trails. After I moved here, I heard about the waterfalls. I wanted to go on a hunt for them, but before I did, I had to take a trip to Grand Rapids, Michigan, for work. There I was, surrounded by some of the wisest, most intelligent individuals. Scholars with lots of degrees. As someone who repeated fifth grade and never went to college, I was both intimidated and inspired by how they processed information. My brain just doesn't operate that way. And I felt unqualified. I had to keep fighting the lie that I was unqualified to be in the positions I was in and unqualified to speak on certain topics. But in my vulnerable state, I reminded myself over and over, God *loves* the unqualified. That is where he shows up. So, I kept looking up to him and asking him to replace my swirling thoughts of feeling unqualified.

The comparison trap had a field day that week. Even when I got home, those insecurities started to manifest again. I had to shush them away and tell myself, *Well, Eryn, at least you were brave about what you did not know, and that's something to be proud of.*

The next morning, I woke with this inner stirring to find those waterfalls. It was like God was saying, *Hey, make some coffee, put your boots on, and let's go for a walk.* So, I did exactly that. I rushed out the door and took off down the trails, only to check myself as I realized I was rushing instead of being in the moment. I wanted to listen to God's thoughts and reconnect with how he saw me and not how I saw me or even how other people saw me.

So, I slowed my pace, watched the trees blow in the wind, took deep breaths, and prayed, "God, reveal what you think of me. Help me replace all these insecurities with your thoughts."

As I approached the waterfall, my breath began to slow, as did my thoughts. The comparison spiral was coming to a stop. I was beginning to recognize the lies I had been telling myself and to see God's truth about me. But I needed to pause and be still with these thoughts.

As I sat down on the bench perched in front of the waterfall, I noticed a concrete slab underneath me. I brushed my feet to move the leaves and uncovered a metal plate that read,

Be still and know that I am God.

Be still and know.

Be still.

Be.

Wow. Okay, God. I get it. I need to be still and be still in you.

I could not believe it. He cared about me so much that he led me to a place of rest to remind me that I need to be still and know that he is God. He is good, and because I am made in his image, I am good. He is love. And by his Son, who died for me, I am loved. He is enough, and I don't need to be anything to anyone. I am enough.

These days, you often hear people say they are learning to live by their truth. But the truth is, their truth could be wearing a mask of lies. What they believe is true could be a lie dressed as truth, like my truth was. Our truth is not actually ours. God is the only one who can be totally true. The only way to know what is true is to go to the source of truth. The source of love. And to be still in the source.

In Jeremiah 29:11 (KJV), God says, "For I know the thoughts that I think toward you." Don't you want to know what they are? I do. The source of love and the source of truth knows the thoughts that he thinks of us, and they are truer than we could ever hope for.

According to Isaiah 43:4, God sees me as precious in his eyes, and honored, and he loves me. My creator, my inventor, the maker of my DNA—my hair texture, my unique fingerprints, my eye

BE STILL AND KNOW
THAT I AM GOD.
BE STILL AND KNOW.
BE STILL.
BE.

color, and my awkward birthmarks—sees me as precious in his eyes.

Here are a few more truths:

I am utterly secure in him; nothing will be able to separate me from his love in Christ Jesus. (Rom. 8:39)

No one is able to snatch me out of his hand. (John 10:29)

He will never leave me nor forsake me. (Heb. 13:5)

While I know what he says about me, and I can read Scripture until I am blue in the face, I want to believe it. I want his beliefs about me to be my beliefs. I want *his* truth to be my truth. Our actions that come from his beliefs about us will lead to our healing and dancing in freedom, knowing that no performance will gain us any more love, because we are already loved. We are made by *the* One who invented love, the One who invented truth, and the truth is, we are *loved* because we are made by the image of Love.

Living in the truth that he loves you is a continual, never-arrive, always-fight-for-it kind of journey. It gets easier over time, but rarely is it easy. Nothing worth it is easy.

The enemy studies us and discovers what our biggest fears are, and then he goes on a mission to confirm them. The enemy uses people who are good as well as people who are hurtful to accomplish that. We must learn to disrupt our thoughts with the question, *God, what do you think?*

If you want to live a life that is free from the lies you think are true and experience the love God has for you, ask him to replace your lies with his beliefs. Set reminders on your phone throughout the day of his truth to rewire where your brain goes. Your actions follow your beliefs. And if your beliefs are his beliefs, you will walk in his truth and live a life free from lies.

This journey to learning who God is will be the biggest adventure of your life. And just as he directed my journey to the waterfall, so will he direct your path in this life. He wants that invitation from us, and he wants to teach us how to accept his grace and love. He wants to teach us how to live in the freedom of knowing we are beautiful and good and enough. I tell God often, "You have brought light to my life; my God, you light up my darkness. You delight in me; I know you do because you say so, and you only speak truth. I will believe that truth."

To matter means to be of importance. I matter to God and God matters to me. And you matter to God. Does he matter to you?

He is what we are searching for and what we can't seem to get enough of anywhere else. No amount of money, clothes, or success will satisfy the thirst to be loved and to be seen. He is what we desire. He is what we want. We want an indefinite amount of love and worth, and he *is that*.

Let him matter to you because you always have and always will matter to him.

Hear him say, *Calm your thoughts. Look up at me. See in my eyes that you are more and far greater than your imagination could ever take you to wonder. You can become far more than your limitations will allow you to believe. See in my eyes, beloved. You are mine, and that is enough. I'm so proud of you, and every door I open before you, I hope you gracefully accept. I delight in your faithfulness to know me. Be still and unafraid.*

breath prayer

Lord, I pray that you will guard my heart. I pray that you will replace my thoughts with your thoughts. Lord, I pray that you will intervene with truth. I pray that your voice will be loud. Louder than the lies I have been living in. I want to know what you think of me, Jesus. Amen.

Healing

heal·ing | \ˈhēl-iŋ\
restoring to health, becoming well

When I moved into a new apartment, I had six boxes full of clothes from my past life that I just didn't wear anymore. Some of them were gifts from an ex, some reminded me of *that* date night, when I left feeling icky, and some carried other bad memories.

I didn't want to unpack them, so they sat there forever. One night, instead of dealing with them, I found myself wandering from my closet to my desk, where I hopped on Facebook. The first thing I saw were those old memories that pop up on your feed. You know, the ones that say, "On this day . . ." I ended up doing a different kind of cleaning out that night . . . I deleted all my old photos.

I looked back at my old photos and saw a girl who was found, lost, lost, found, lost again, found, and then healed. I pinballed back and forth from being found, knowing God loved me and nothing else mattered for validation, to being lost, feeling unlovable and seeking outside attention, to finally being heard, aware of all of it and continually being mended, recovered, restored, rehabilitated, and repaired.

Being healed means I accept the Healer's love for me. It does not mean I will never struggle. It does not mean I will never become unmended. It does not mean I am fixed or I have arrived. In that specific moment, comparing the photos of my old lost self to my present, healed self, I saw someone who had accepted and received God's love. And as I continue to learn, I will continue to evolve.

Our choices lead to healing, and our bodies are a reflection of the mending God is doing in us. I can see my choices and my lifestyle changes reflected in my eyes.

Matthew 6:22–23 (NIV) says, "The eye is the lamp of the body. If your eyes are healthy, your whole body will be full of light. But if your eyes are unhealthy, your whole body will be full of darkness."

Maybe it was dramatic to delete old photos. But it felt really good to see the light in my eyes and to identify a distinct difference between the old Eryn and the new. Let your eyes be the proof. If you're like me, you pray to God over and over to show you what he sees. Don't forget to look in the mirror sometimes; you might smile at what you see. And if you're still struggling to see the light come back, ask him to let it show up in your eyes.

In August 2018, my dad had a cancer scare. He began losing his voice on and off. My dad's voice is usually raspy, but now it sounded like a whisper. The doctors found something dark on his esophagus, quickly took a biopsy, and went ahead and scheduled him for radiation treatment. While we waited, we did everything we could to discipline our minds from going to worst-case scenarios.

The biopsy came back clear. He was fine. They told him to keep an eye on it, gave him medication for acid reflux, and said he was good to go. A year later, he had the same problem, but worse. This time, pain accompanied his voicelessness. So we did all those things over again. Biopsy, scheduling, waiting. This time, when the tests came back, my dad had cancer. The doctor gave him two choices: he could have surgery and never have his voice again, or he could have radiation, which would significantly impact his thyroid but salvage his voice. He chose the voice.

Five days a week for three months, I watched my dad fight for healing. To treat throat cancer, they burn your neck from the outside in. I watched my dad fight with such emotional strength as his body reflected so much pain. It got worse before it got better, but finally, by October, there was no more cancer. He was healed. He still had to deal with debris from the fight, but the source of pain that threatened his life was gone.

Healing does not mean we have arrived. Healing means we walk closer to the source that can remedy the big hurdles in life that we don't have enough strength to fight on our own. Was my dad scared? Yes. Absolutely. My dad went through a long list of burdens . . . regrets about things he wished he could do differently, worries about how his kids would be if this took him home to heaven, fears about whether or not my mom would be okay. He was scared, but his fear wasn't as strong as his faith.

He looked at it this way: faith and fear are two sides of the same coin. They are both about believing in the unknown. You have to decide which road you're going to take. Faith isn't an easy road, but it is the very thing that will hold you up and give you strength. Faith is giving up your compulsion to do what feels good and instead learning what is actually good for you. And learning Who is good, always.

Faith is uncomfortable, but the more you practice it and explore it, the more comfortable it gets. Faith is something you build in relationship with God. Faith is knowing God will show up to recover your circumstances and heal your heart over and over again. Faith doesn't mean knowing all the answers. It can even be scary when you're faced with questions you can't answer about God, and in those times, I've leaned into the proof of what God has healed in me to affirm that to live by faith is a far better choice than to live in fear.

If the choice is faith or fear, which path are you going to take? May we desire the path of faith. For the path of faith leads to healing, and healing is the proof that God is bigger than we ever thought.

breath prayer

Lord, I pray that you will reveal to me what path I have been choosing. I want to live a life of faith and not fear, but I don't always know how to. Reveal in me the questions I have but am too scared to ask. Please guide my feet to a life dependent on your guidance, that you would lead me to the areas of my heart that need healing, the areas that I have yet to notice. Amen.

Loneliness

lone·li·ness | \'lōn-lē-nəs\
sadness because one has no friends or company

I think there are two kinds of loneliness. The first is when you're in a room full of people but still feel completely alone. Have you experienced that?

I remember attending a Christmas party four years ago. I can picture it so vividly. I was surrounded by people: friends, acquaintances, even some strangers. Yet I felt all alone. I went home feeling more empty than seen. More isolated than I'd felt even before the party. But why? By definition, *loneliness* is sadness because one has no friends or company, yet I think we can feel loneliness despite proximity to people. Even people we love. Even people who love us.

After some much-needed heart attention, I realized my loneliness didn't stem from the number of people or the kind of people in my life; it was rooted in my chosen perspective at that time.

I felt extremely insecure and didn't really like myself much. It didn't matter if the room was full of people who had only nice things to say about me. I wouldn't have believed them anyway because, in that season, I didn't have any nice things to say about me.

But what about the other kind of loneliness—when you didn't even get invited to the party? I've been there too. During my divorce, as people picked sides, the invitations I used to hang on my refrigerator slowly faded from many to some . . . to none. I saw pictures of my ex on social media attending the parties we used to go to together. I was no longer included in group texts that used to include me. The slow drip of loneliness quickly became a first-class ticket to insecurity land.

Maybe for you, loneliness didn't manifest in the fallout of a divorce. Maybe it was the death of a loved one or the first holiday after a breakup. Maybe you moved to a new city or experienced the falling out of a friendship. Or maybe you felt that first kind of loneliness, where you're surrounded but still utterly alone. It doesn't matter where it comes from, the presence of loneliness inevitably leads to the question, *Am I not enough?*

This next part might sound crazy, but hang with me.

Loneliness caused me many bleak days filled with more darkness than joy, but without it, I'm not sure I would have ever understood how brutally—dare I say abusively—I viewed myself. This sounds obvious, but the ache of loneliness helped me see how lonely I was inside. It brought up questions and emotions I didn't even know were buried deep down, and it provided me space to process them.

Being alone gives us the opportunity to honestly assess whether or not we feel lonely. And if so, to explore why.

Through my experience, I've come to see loneliness as a gift.

We can be alone and find contentment with who we are. Many people think I am an extrovert, but I definitely recharge by talking to my plants, not people. Alone time used to be scary. When I didn't like me, being alone felt like a living hell. It was really lonely. But now I like my alone time because I've learned to like myself.

Author Chip Dodd says, "Sometimes we learn in loneliness to put our sword and shield down and cry our guts out about the battles we've waged and lost—dreams and hopes not fulfilled, friends missed, intimacies not honored, opportunities not taken and struggles with God not seen through."[2]

You may feel really lonely right now, and honestly, there are no magic words I can say to remove the painful residue left on your heart. But I hope my words provide some relief and assurance that what you're experiencing is completely normal. I have found comfort by just knowing that I am not alone in what feels like my deep well of loneliness.

Chip Dodd goes on to say, "By struggling in solitude, we eventually rekindle the passion that led us into battle in the first place."[3]

Can I share a quick tip that helped me survive my loneliness? Acknowledge how you feel, and let yourself dream. Journal what you desire, what you hope for.

One especially lonely evening, I put on one of my favorite movies—*Ever After* with Drew Barrymore—and I made a secret Pinterest board. I called it "Eryn 2.0." I had three categories in it: (1) My Closet, (2) My Home, and (3) My Business.

I went to town dreaming on these boards when I was lonely. Instead of being stuck in the comparison trap, these boards inspired me to dream of what I hoped to see. My modern-day vision board gave me a little boost of confidence and something to look forward to as I continued to seek help.

Your inbox may not be full of invites to the big parties of the season, which I know is truly hurtful and hard. Or maybe you dread going to those parties because they make you feel even more alone, which is equally hard and scary. Those feelings aren't a reflection of who you are or what you're worth.

God promises to carry the weight of loneliness and fill the emptiness in our hearts. In fact, he's waiting for an invite from you. And trust me, it'll be the best one you ever send.

2. Chip Dodd, *The Voice of the Heart* (Nashville: Sage Hill, 2001), 50.
3. Dodd, *The Voice of the Heart*, 51.

breath prayer

Lord, I invite you in. I pray that you will fill the emptiness in my heart. Lord, in my moments of searching and disbelief, would you show me your love and influence in my life? I ask that you reveal more of yourself to me. Amen.

Relief

re·lief | \ri-ˈlēf\
removal of something oppressive, painful, or distressing

After my divorce, I had a business deal go south. With the accumulated debt from those two events, on paper I was worth roughly negative $160,000. Not to mention the $25,000 in back rent I owed on office space. Let me just say, this particular cocktail of debt, heartbreak, and poor decisions was quite potent.

All I could do was ask, *When will there be relief?* Maybe you've wondered the same thing. Or maybe you're wondering it right now.

I remember a January day when I was met with the slow beginning of relief. I rarely checked my Facebook messages, but one day when I did, I found a message in my inbox from a man named Jim. We had been Facebook friends for some time, and he was doing a clean sweep of friends for the sake of the New Year. He wanted to connect with friends he had yet to meet. I was one of them. He sent me a very brief message saying, "I don't normally do this, but we have a lot of mutual friends, we're in the same line of work, and I think we should meet." Little did I know I would sit across from a man who would help me understand the extent of my disbelief in myself.

I showed up to the meeting not sure what to expect. I knew we had mutual friends and he was in a community of socially conscious brands with the desire to do good, so I knew we'd have something to talk about.

The previous night, I had been feeling the weight of my circumstances, but that morning, I masked it with a thick coat of foundation, bright red lipstick, and a $200 leather hat from the Goorin Brothers. I walked in with a pep in my step that looked more like denial, and I shared my vision and what I was doing with my business. The truth is, I wasn't doing much. I had taken a year off and had been crawling out of that financial hole of debt, healing the divorce wounds, and feeling pretty purposeless.

As I shared my story with my mask on, Jim stayed intrigued, asking questions to learn more. I had some really great points and, as a visionary would have, a great argument for why my So Worth Loving idea should exist and where I wanted to take it. Then he asked the question, "I know what you want to do, but where is the company currently at?"

(*Crickets . . .*)

I had no answer. I sat across from him and had no choice but to take the mask off. "This is where it is, Jim. I am in debt. I carried the financial burden of my household for the last two years of my marriage, I made some terrible business choices, and I'm not really sure how to get out of this, and honestly, I am depressed. I see my dream, but I feel so far away from even being a candidate for it. I don't know how to get there. I don't know where to begin. I just don't know anything anymore. All I know is how to fake it, and that feels pretty depressing too."

Jim looked at me and said, "You have what it takes, and your story is not too far off from what I have had to overcome."

As Jim shared his redemptive story with me, I slowly started to feel the warmth of relief. Maybe I could truly muster up the energy to be a candidate for the dreams I wanted to pursue.

Two weeks before I met with Jim, I had read the Scripture in Matthew 9:17 that says you cannot put new wine into old wineskins. I had prayed that God would make new wine out of my circumstances and, oh, by the way, when I received that message from Jim, I laughed to learn that his last name was Vinyard. Since that day, he has been an ally, a friend, and a believer in me. In my disbelief, Jim gifted me belief, and that gave me so much relief. That's what we all do for each other. I guess I should say I *hope* that is what we all do for each other. Gift each other belief, for that in itself brings so much relief.

Our circumstances don't define who we are at our core, but how we handle them can define who we become. And how we find relief. It's easy to think that if our circumstances and conditions change, then how we feel will change too. While it would have felt great to be debt-free or in a healthy, loving relationship, the truth is . . . it wouldn't have provided me lasting relief because it wouldn't have changed how I viewed myself deep down.

If you're stuck, in need of recovery or even a miracle, relief won't always come the way you want it to . . . quickly or swiftly. Relief comes when you work through the muck and mess, when you remain disciplined in your thinking, and when you constantly practice the act of surrendering. Only then will you see a miracle. When you work through the natural consequences of reckless behavior or ignorance or whatever it was that landed you in your current circumstances (and maintain your sanity through the process), that is a miracle. And you should be proud of yourself!

You develop confidence and find relief when you acknowledge the work you've done and celebrate the little victories. It often takes painful circumstances for us to face the root issue . . . how we see ourselves. Relief is owning the consequences and not allowing your emotions to be controlled by them.

Relief didn't look at all like I thought it would. It didn't come in the form of being debt-free or getting my credit score out of the tank. It didn't come from maintaining a healthy relationship or having a long list of people who liked me.

Relief came when I stopped allowing the phone calls from debt collectors to dictate my emotions. And when I stopped letting checks from freelance projects affect my internal worth.

Relief came when I quit listening to the shame of my mistakes. And when I forgave myself and all the people who made me feel unworthy and unloved.

Relief came when I got on my knees and asked Jesus to make something new from this mess I found myself in. And when I was able to say, "This is yours, Lord. It's yours now . . . we've done the work of acceptance, ownership, and healing. I am now doing my best. This is yours. Make a way, Jesus."

No person and no circumstance could have provided the kind of relief I needed. Relief came from slowly and gracefully confronting my reality. It takes a kind of bravery to face the things we struggle with, but doing so is the only way to experience the weightlessness of relief. It takes courage to face yourself and love yourself through the process.

If you find yourself in immeasurable pressure and heartache, know that it will pass. Be kind to yourself. Drink more water than wine, and say no more often than yes. You will find your stride, I promise. I pray you will see yourself the way God sees you and not through the lens of your circumstances and conditions.

That's where relief is found.

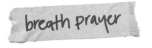

Lord, my _____ (finances, career, relationship with X) feel(s) so unsteady, but I know you are a God of providing relief. If the birds have food, so will I be cared for. I pray that you will show up with relief in places where I am stumbling. I love you, Father. Amen.

Choose

choose | \'chüz\
to make a final choice, embrace, accept

I am often overwhelmed by the idea that God *chose* me. He didn't have to, but he loves me so much that he chose to be inflicted with unbearable pain, leading to his death. He voluntarily chose to absorb judgment, doubt, denial, betrayal, anger, greed, lust, self-ishness. He chose to absorb physical pain, disease, illness, injury. He grabbed all of it, endured it, and demonstrated his love for me. For you.

During the time when I was pretty far away from talking to God, I hadn't read my Bible in a while. I probably couldn't have even told you where it was. My Bible had my old last name—my married name—on it, and I didn't care to read that last name on the cover. But I didn't care to read anything I might find on the inside either. My community of friends took sides during my divorce, and I was now the outcast. Most of them associated themselves with God, which frankly made the concept of me leaning into God during this time seem like a far cry. I allowed the enemy to get in and warp the way I viewed God and the way I believed God viewed me.

At the time, I was helping a company called Worship Circle with their branding and social media. Worship Circle is a mentoring program for worship leaders, and every year they put on a retreat to help worship leaders feel less alone in their struggles. I went to the retreat to help document it. On the last night, everyone in attendance took Communion. If you're unfamiliar, Communion is the symbolic representation of Jesus dying on the cross. Usually someone reads what Jesus said to his disciples on the eve of his death, and then we eat a piece of bread to represent his body being given over to sin. Then we drink wine (or grape juice, depending on where you are) as a symbol of his blood that was poured out in the name of love.

I've taken Communion hundreds of times. But this time was different. I was emotionally tired, in debt, living a life of fear, and being driven by a scarcity mindset. But the environment in this room felt safe. I could feel the verse I clung to, the words of Matthew 11:28, in the air: "Are you tired? Worn out? Burned out on religion? Come to me. Get away with me and you'll recover your life. I'll show you how to take a real rest."

The room was full of singing voices that expressed their burnout, and yet I felt their desire to give God the weight, and in that moment, they did. As I sat there, even as numb to the world as I was, I thought, *I want what they have. I want an open heart, a surrendered heart.* For the first time in a long time, I wanted to say, "Okay, God, I'll try to trust you."

As I closed my eyes and let the voices fill the room, God gave me the most beautiful vision: Jesus nailed to a tree, his body completely destroyed, hurting and bleeding with thorns on his head, a blurred crowd mocking him. You could feel the denial and betrayal.

As I stood in the back of the crowd, I heard Jesus call to me. "Eryn, come here. Come to me." So I walked up to him. As I looked up at him, my face full of shame, he said, "Look in my eyes. You are worth every bit of the love I have for you. All the people whose terrible words have hurt you don't know what they're saying. Their opinions don't matter, and their words will fall flat when you learn to live a life that reflects my love. All the words spoken over you will be replaced as you give each word to me to wear. Let me wash away all that you see in your past. You are worthy, child. You are worthy of this. I choose this pain because I chose you."

I hope to always keep that vision in my mind. I can still see it with my eyes wide open. It left such an impression on my heart. It changed me. I surrendered to choose God and believe he was good; there are just some not-so-good people that represent his name, but that is not the same thing.

I hope you will go back and reread the section above, replacing my name with yours. He chose you, too, and he is waiting for you to choose him. He wants to carry the weight of your questions, guilt, shame, fears, and doubts. He wants to work things out with you. He does not want you to work things out by yourself. We just aren't strong enough. And please hear me. I am not diminishing our capabilities . . . our skills, our talents. I just recognize that physical abuse, sexual abuse, emotional abuse, disease, deception, self-mutilation, disorders, heartbreak, loneliness, lies, chemical imbalances, and death are too heavy for us to handle in our own power. On the cross, he wore all those things for us, and we can trust that any terrible thing we have done or said—he wore that too. He saw our reckless and afflicted state and matched it with his reckless love.

Being fully seen and fully myself, and loved more for it, is the biggest adventure I've ever been on. It's the most beautiful romance I've ever been a part of. While I still have trust issues and I'm still healing from trauma, I feel God's presence fighting along with me every day. Instead of squeezing my fists tighter around my issues, I know I can call upon him at any point in my day and give them over to him. I thought it was too good to be true. But I was wrong; it's so true.

A relationship with God is an adventure of discovering who we are and how to live out the purpose he has for us. Every day, I am changing. I discover more of what I desire and what he thinks about those desires. Every day, the more I stay close to him, the

I AM CHOOSING
TO BE FULLY SEEN
AND FULLY MYSELF
(AND) AM LOVED
MORE FOR IT.

more I am impacted by his love. I discover how willing he is to listen to my questions and how ready he is to receive the struggles and burdens I am carrying. Every day, I uncover a little bit more about how he views me.

And that's what I want for you. Because he didn't just choose me. He chose you too. You, who are so worth loving.

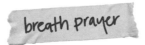

Lord, you are my choice. You are the only consistent presence in my life worth fighting for. The relationship worth fighting to protect. I pray that I will see myself the way you see me. That I will see you choose to pursue me every day because I am worth it. Lord, you say I am worthy. You always have. I invite you into my life, and I choose to live an unexplainable life with you in it. I know you will never leave me. May I continue to learn about that radical love you have for me and be a walking example of your love for others to know. Amen.

LOOK OUT

---

embracing your past and empowering your future

If there is one thing I've learned in owning So Worth Loving, it is the power of story. Not just the courage of sharing what your story is, but that there is a power that comes from being present in your own story. It is being in the presence of our story that impacts our communities. Because the truth is, the more we become comfortable with our story, the more grace we have for someone else learning to understand theirs. Discovering your true value is not prim and proper. It's messy. Oftentimes it involves wrong turns and more questions than answers.

As you have discovered more of your story throughout this book, there may have been times (if not the whole time) when you felt invisible. Hidden. There have been moments when I've felt invisible. I've felt so much emotion through cycles of grief that I thought those around me might not understand, but your feeling of being invisible may eventually give visibility to those around you. Our story not only impacts us and the trajectory of our future, but it also empowers someone else in their story. Through feeling unknown, you will be able to walk others through their pain and help them to feel known.

I think that is why being so incredibly present with your story is crucial. It's not just about you; it is also about others. If we are to love our neighbors as we love ourselves, it starts with the presence of ourselves in our story.

Can you recall a time when you were faithless and there were people to lean on whose faith you could borrow? Once we've grieved, we can sit with someone else who is grieving, and we will know what to do, what not to do, and how to walk them toward discovering their value because we, too, have been there.

When I looked out, I still felt I was carrying some weight, and I learned I was waiting for God to fully heal me of my past. While I feel he continues to recover my career, my thoughts, my relationships . . . I also learned that discovering your value never ends. You evolve in learning more about it. You learn how to enjoy the sweet taste of a new outlook and, for some of us, a new beginning. Grieving your past is not a sign that you're weak or that you do not have enough faith. You move forward with grief as a companion, and you learn to shame yourself less and less when the waves of it come in. You learn to love others with a deep-found capacity. You learn that your healing is significant not just for you but also for your neighbors. Your friends. Your family. Your loved ones.

Once you've been fully present in your own life, looking in and looking up to face the pain, to grieve, and to turn to God, you have a different outlook and a different way of approaching everything around you. You can read the eyes and the smiles in a room and know what's really going on in someone's life. You can look out and know, and you can help someone feel known. You can see because you lived every feeling that it took to discover your true value.

As you have asked the hard questions, revealed lies, allowed yourself to be angry, and learned how God sees you, most likely

OUR STORY NOT
ONLY IMPACTS US
(AND) THE
TRAJECTORY
OF OUR FUTURE,

BUT (IT) ALSO
EMPOWERS
SOMEONE ELSE
IN THEIR STORY.

you've started to notice some things changing around you. You may not talk about the same things or do the same things you used to. You may not mesh as well as you used to with some of your friends. Friends may even feel a little awkward around you because your ways are changing and theirs aren't. Only rare and special friendships last through all seasons without threatening the depth of respect and love you have for each other.

In this section, my hope is to share how, with a newfound knowledge, you can trust yourself again, learn to desire more for your life, reflect on your friendships and become a better friend, forgive those who have never apologized, and help your friends and family feel more known as they walk through discovering their true value like you continue to do.

Consider the courage it took to stay in your story a superpower that now can help someone else feel known.

Breathe

breathe | \\ˈbrēth\\
to be fully alive, to exist

I was seven thousand feet above sea level and it was hard to breathe. I could feel my lungs slowly inhaling and exhaling, asking when I could get to a lower elevation. Did I really have to wait four days before I could breathe normally?

My whole family was spending Christmas in Santa Fe, New Mexico, but I couldn't afford a ticket, so I had planned to stay back and spend time with my grandma. Six days before Christmas, my sister and her husband ended up surprising me with a ticket. I was so thankful. I thought I'd worn out my welcome as the family member who cries all the time and can't give anyone anything for Christmas because she is *broke*. But that didn't stop them from welcoming me with open arms! I was at my lowest and still loved.

Being at a high altitude wasn't bad; my body just wasn't used to it. Walking around, I felt a little delirious, so I went to an oxygen bar, which is exactly what it sounds like—a bar that sells oxygen—and eventually got acclimated. I knew going from Georgia to New Mexico would be a different experience, but I also knew this trip was exactly what I needed. And what my family needed, despite my messiness. I needed their tangible love, and they needed practice loving a heartbreak.

Altitude can be defined as the distance above the horizon. And *horizon* can be defined as the limit of a person's range of experience.

Sometimes it takes other people, with their knowledge and experience, to help us see beyond our own horizons. Our temptation may be to self-isolate or hide, but other people are the way we learn to adapt to our new life. They help our breathing get acclimated to our new view. Our new way of living. Our new way of loving. The way they love others and the way they love us can teach us how to love and live.

Who around you has a range of experiences beyond yours? Who around you can offer a different view?

If it's true we are the sum of the five people we hang out with most, then who are those people and what are their characteristics? What do we admire about them? What inspires us about them? What are their careers like? How do they love their family? Friends? God?

Our temptation is to feed our appetite for acceptance. It's easier to surround ourselves with people who accept us than it is to protect ourselves from those we're surrounded by. People from a higher altitude of experience will challenge you. They will make things uncomfortable. But there is discovery in our discomfort if we lean into it. The more uncomfortable we become, the more likely we are to unearth areas of our hearts in need of tending.

Are you willing to invite discomfort? The more we subject ourselves to discomfort, the more we discover how we respond to it, which allows us to grow from it.

A couple years ago, I started working part-time for Gwinnett Church. By the grace of God, this job came into my life. I felt pretty jaded about the church. So, of course, God placed me in a job at a church.

I'll never forget the first staff meeting. I went to the bathroom twice so I could sit, fully clothed, on the toilet and just breathe.

My chest felt so tight. I didn't realize being around so many people who loved God would make me feel so uncomfortable. I mean, I thought I loved God too. I knew I was cynical, but I didn't think being around the church, whom I deemed judgmental Christians, would bother me to that extent.

When I say "the church," I don't necessarily mean the physical building but the group of individuals who identify as believing in Jesus, God, and the Holy Spirit.

I've made it very apparent in this book that I cared what everybody thought about me, but I cared the most about what other Christians thought. I confused their views with God's view. And while my attitude said, "I do not care," the fact is, I harbored the most animosity toward people who identified as Christian. Anger reveals what we do care about, what we're attempting to deny.

Though Gwinnett Church was a physical building, it was made up of people who helped me regain my trust of Christ followers. They represented what the church should be . . . people so aware of God's love and mercy for them that they understand they have no right to project judgment. They could see God was transforming my heart, and while they weren't about to get in the way, they knew they wanted to be a part of the journey.

But let me be very honest . . . I was so uncomfortable at staff meetings and creative meetings. It took a lot of deep breaths from my diaphragm for me to cope with the anxiety. I was defensive and prideful. I was so afraid of being judged that I protected myself by not engaging. I just kept my head down. I gave just enough of what they needed. Somehow I did not lose my job. They kept renewing my contract, and they kept loving me. They kept showing me my talent and my skill by asking me to speak into the direction of projects. Their love showed me who I was and who I could be.

Discomfort in the presence of the right people showed me who I could be comfortable with. Who was safe. What God thought of me. When you're in a valley, you feel lost, staring up at the mountain, wondering how the heck you're going to get to the top—or even halfway there. But when you finally climb to seven thousand feet above sea level, you will struggle to breathe . . . to take deep breaths, to embrace the beauty, and to give thanks for what you see. Sometimes the valley feels safer than struggling to acclimate your breath to your new view. You might even start to desire the valley because the mountaintop moment is uncomfortable. The healing process leads to relief, but you may feel undeserving.

I'm learning contentment doesn't come from a change of circumstances. Contentment comes from our perspective of our circumstances. It's about how we frame our view. How we exist inside our circumstances. You can be just as overwhelmed on top of a mountain as you are in a valley. In a valley, you can be afraid of all you have yet to overcome. While on top of the mountain, you can look down on all you've already overcome but fear that you might fall off.

But fear is not of God. The voice of fear wants to keep you from being fully alive. Let your breath get acclimated to the new view. And if you're in a valley, embrace what you see and be thankful for what it's doing to your heart, to your character. Life is an ebb and flow of valleys and mountaintops. I'm learning to see beauty in both and to be fully alive in both.

How do you feel about your current circumstances? How can you shift your perspective, listening to the voice of love rather than the voice of fear? Have you experienced discomfort in the presence of the right people? Journal about what that's looked like in your life.

Risk

risk | \'risk\
exposure to possible loss or injury

Risk is a teacher. As an entrepreneur, I am no stranger to risk. I guess that comes with the territory. I've signed leases and contracts and made promises about new endeavors without having any idea if I could actually pull them off. Without risk, we don't get to see what we are made of. Without risk, we remain isolated and safe. Never stepping out of our comfort zone. Never putting into practice the knowledge that God is who he says he is.

We will never get to fully see him without risk.

To grow into a new way of living, we have to take a risk and put our hearts out there. When we have the right people around us, people who are for us, God will use that safe community to show us we are seen by him. But what happens if we have been burned by our community? How do we risk being vulnerable again?

When I jumped into the dating scene after my divorce, I did not have healthy boundaries, and I did not have many people around me I could call to ask questions about how to do this thing: *How do I honor my body and my mind? How do I not get too ahead of myself? If I travel with a guy, do we stay in different hotel rooms? His relationship with his mom is like X; what do I think of that? I feel this way; is that fear or discernment?* I talked to my therapist about these questions, but he was expensive. I needed friendships I could lean on for sound advice.

If I could do it again, I would have rebuilt my community first and then slowly stepped into dating. Instead, I dove into dating, only to realize I didn't have any community.

I'm probably preaching to the choir, but if you've ever been through a circumstance that caused most of the people in your life to step away, you know it's really hard to learn how to trust as you step back into friendships and relationships. You don't really trust anyone, let alone yourself.

When we are far from God or feel he is nowhere to be found, he uses people in our lives to be physical representations of his love. When we are terrified to talk about our struggles, God uses people to be the bridge and sit with us.

For a couple years, I was pretty shy about involving myself publicly in any type of ministry work. I was letting shame direct my steps. So, when I got a call from one of the most influential Christian organizations in the world asking me to do an interview, it'd be an understatement to say I was uncertain of my place there.

Whenever I recognize any automatic negative thoughts, I try to surrender them, but that doesn't stop them from paying me visits every now and then. I've learned to cope with these statements instead of just ignoring them.

As I approached this interview, the negative thoughts were becoming more and more frequent. Some of them even came in the form of things people had said to me years before regarding my faith. I heard things like . . .

> *"You should not be on stages to normalize divorce for young Christian girls."*
>
> *"A woman of God does not divorce her husband."*
>
> *"When you get to heaven, will you be able to look God in the eyes?"*

I didn't realize these words had left such a sting until I took a risk and stepped back into those same environments. As inaccurate and condemning as those words were, that didn't stop them from popping up unwelcome throughout the day of my interview. All day, I wondered if these new people, as they got to know me more, would start to agree with the people from my past. If I was vulnerable with this ministry, would they confirm what were obviously still unhealed wounds in my mind?

I made it through without letting shame or fear control my thoughts or words. Partly because, just like the people at Gwinnett Church, the people at this organization didn't judge me either. They loved me. They were kind to me. They ended up helping me heal those wounds and restore my thoughts.

That is the beauty of risk. I stepped into an environment where I could have been met with more hurt and disappointment. But instead, I was met with understanding. And even if the outcome had been different, if they had become another condemning voice, the fact that I was brave enough to enter into an environment that reminded me of past pain revealed a lot to me. It showed me I had enough courage to move forward and had experienced more healing than I gave myself credit for.

As you take risks, remember to give yourself credit. Identify the areas where you've been scared to take risks. Maybe there are some things you've belittled about yourself that actually represent a big feat for you. My guess is that you've experienced growth and your past self would be proud of the areas where you've handled things in a new way. Celebrate those victories, even if they feel small. Acknowledge and tell yourself, *I had more confidence than I realized despite the outcome.* Confidence is developed when we have the willingness to take risks.

How can you establish safe community as you take a risk and enter back into meaningful relationships? Ask God to show you the areas of your heart that still need tending, and pray for people to come into your life who will help tend to those vulnerabilities.

LOOK OUT

Desire

de·sire | \di-ˈzī(-ə)r\
a strong wish, a formal request for action

Do you think desire is a good thing? Have you been told it is bad? Sinful? Sexual? When you hear the word *desire*, what is the first thing that comes to mind?

Desire is good! Desiring more for our life is *good*! Appetite is good! Having a thirst and hunger to do something that makes us excited and satisfied is *good*! But as the saying goes, too much of a good thing is not good anymore, and if we do not know where our appetite is taking us by the ingredients that make it up, it can do more harm than good.

I want to talk about two types of desire in particular: self-seeking desire and good desire. Our self-seeking desire is to satisfy whatever we are hungry for in the moment, and then we have our good, God-seeking desire, which is filled with curiosity, adventure, and a longing for healing for ourselves and others.

Desire is the central point of our very being that communicates with the Holy Spirit; it's a place for us to hear him. Deep down in our core, our desire is God's desire. Since we are made in his image, and God desires for us to live a fulfilling, forgiving, grace-extending, mercy-receiving, loving life, you'd better believe your desires at the core are far more beautiful and adventurous than anything you could ever conjure up on your own.

I want to be careful talking about our self-seeking desires. Let us not mistake self-seeking desires for things we want at our core that we feel led to do or hope to one day achieve. Self-seeking desires are ones that are built on the appetite of always wanting more because we have empty spaces in us that are made up of pain from our past. Those spaces are caused by wounds we have not tended to or wounds that are freshly healing. Self-seeking desires are typically led by deprivation, abandonment, fear, insecurity, heartbreak, or the desire for attention. They come from the desire to be seen and known by the outside world for validation that we are good, smart, funny, or pretty. If we can satisfy ourselves long enough, we will enjoy life until we need another hit of validation, and we will grab at anything that is physically around us and seek validation from it. However, we are meant to grab hold of our Creator and seek validation from him instead. Can you imagine how less tired you would be if you sought the Creator, who promises to give you rest, over others, who give you a quick fix but still leave you feeling restless?

Have you ever found yourself begging God to just tell you what is next? Maybe your anxiety is high, and you feel as though your life is in complete disarray: bills are due, you're dealing with the illness of one of your kids, the doctor's reports came back with bad news. Or maybe you just found out your husband is cheating on you or that a girlfriend has been lying. Maybe you recognize that your rage toward others is out of control. Or your parents got a divorce and it has thrown the dynamic in your family completely off, leaving you with the pressure to put things back together and make things better. You just want to know if you are going to be okay. In those low moments, we grab hold of things that make us feel instantly better. Cue the unknowing, unaddressed appetite that has made a home inside of you.

When pain is unbearable, we seek to make ourselves instantly feel better. So, we grab hold of any friend who will listen, despite their trustworthiness, or we drink too much in order to numb the pain. We watch porn to escape, or we treat sex like it is easy and an act that is solely for gain and pleasure. We go to a psychic to find comfort in our future, or we review our horoscopes in hopes of a better today.

Can you blame anyone for wanting quick relief? No. Life can get so confusing. If you turn on the news and read about the injustice happening all over the world, that alone will make you more depressed than your life itself does. It just applies more layers to sadness and despair. We start to do things outside of our character in the midst of acknowledging the depravity of life. We just want to feel better. I've had my share of not-so-classy, unhealthy, and unwise choices in hopes of finding relief from the hurt that was within me. I've been working through my own negative inner voices and learning to discern the difference between what is of God and what is of fear, and for the longest time, I never believed there was a difference.

The engine that runs the self-seeking desires tells us if we have X, then we will be happy again forever. If we do more of X, we will feel safe again forever. We want to believe it will last forever, but then that brief happiness wears off and we are seeking another vice to perpetuate the feeling. We start to choose counterfeit things to ward off heartache. While it is good for us to seek our desires and passions, we must make sure we are doing it from a place of healing and not void filling.

Behavior modification is not healing. Behavior modification can lead to healing, but it is not to be confused with being healed from our deep wounds.

There is a voice that reminds us of our mistakes and simultaneously tells us to do a particular thing in order to completely fix the issue, and then that voice says, "Ooh, no . . . why did you do that?" The voice that convinces you to seek a quick fix is the same voice that shames you for choosing the quick fix.

Self-seeking desires can lead to more destruction in our lives because they are rooted in overcompensating for the voice we feel we cannot get away from. The voice that whispers to us those hurtful words of shame and tells us that what we hope for is impossible, and it is our fault. Self-seeking desires can be fear driven. They can be rooted in the dissatisfaction of our life, causing us to seek an escape in porn, malicious gossip, people-pleasing, or unhealthy competition and to overindulge in shopping, relationships, social media, sex, alcohol, or food.

God-seeking desires are those that are from the core of who we are. I think it is so important to remember that our core desires are God's desires because God made us to have desires! God-seeking desires are filled with curiosity and adventure. They are filled with the purest form of laughter. They are experiencing the depths of our skill set and exploring our creativity.

What does that look like currently in your life? What could you do with those desires? Remember that the sky is the limit with what you can do with your life when you trust that your God-given desires are good and worth pursuing.

Does desire feel like a good or a bad thing? How so? Can you identify your desires for your life? Ask God to reveal the desires he has placed in you—desires for a fulfilling, forgiving, grace-extending, mercy-receiving, loving life. Ask him to give you a specific image of what that looks like.

Hope

hope | \ˈhōp\
trust and reliance, desire accompanied by expectation

Are you hopeful? A friend and mentor of mine once said, "Sadness is not the absence of hope." And what she meant was that you can be sad and still have hope. Even in your despair, hope can exist. Even in recognizing your self-seeking desires and the sadness you are trying to cover up, you can still have hope.

To hope is to desire with an expectation for fulfillment. We want to be fulfilled, right? Fulfilled with a sustaining, life-giving-to-ourselves-and-others kind of lifestyle. At my core, I want to be generous with my time, attentive to my friends, and present for my family, but my self-seeking desires can get in the way of that.

If we don't define our desires for ourselves, how will we know to achieve them? How will we know what to limit ourselves to? How will we know the kind of discipline and self-control we need to achieve them?

One day I sat down with my journal, and I wrote to God, *If you want me to trust you with my desires, you are going to have to speak loud. For I don't even know how to trust myself completely, but deep down I do know what I desire for my life, and I need your help revealing that to me. Share with me what kind of relationship*

I want to be in, what kind of friend I want to be known as, and what kind of daughter I hope to be to my mom and dad.

I started defining what I was capable of becoming . . . I started expressing my core desire for myself. It caused me to look at the road I was headed down and to be honest with whether my choices aligned with what I believed I was capable of.

And can you believe that my choices did not line up? *Shocker!* Old ways do not make a new path for me. So, I journaled things I needed to give up. People I needed to prune, jobs I needed to say no to, areas of my life I needed God to show up in. I had more hope for my future and more clarity on what was a God-seeking desire over a self-seeking desire.

Hope that aligns with God's love leads to satisfied fulfillment. A God-seeking desire is a journey not of doing but of knowing more about how God made you and what you are capable of. It is restoring our view of ourselves from the identity we once carried out of shame and choosing a new set of desires that lead us to recovery, to hope. You are worthy of the desires God has planted in you. God wants to reveal them to you, and as he does, you will be refined in the process. During the quiet of refinement, your faith builds a deeper intimacy with him. And a deeper capacity to be present with others regardless of their circumstances. I want to give you hope that through the process of refinement, you are more qualified than before to pursue the very thing God has put on your heart.

As I was regaining hope, Psalm 130:1–6 (CSB) was one of the many Scriptures I journaled:

> Out of the depths I call to you, LORD!
> Lord, listen to my voice;
> let your ears be attentive
> to my cry for help.
>
> LORD, if you kept an account of iniquities,
> Lord, who could stand?

But with you there is forgiveness,
so that you may be revered.

I wait for the LORD; I wait
and put my hope in his word.
I wait for the Lord
more than watchmen for the morning.

I cried out and waited, and I hoped. And he listened.

Spend some time writing about your hopes for yourself. Do your choices align with what you believe you're capable of? Are there things or people you need to say no to? Ask God to reveal a sense of hope for the expectations that he will fulfill as you align yourself with his love.

Forgive

for·give | \fər-ˈgiv\
stop feeling angry or resentful toward someone for an
offense, flaw, or mistake

I used to think forgiving someone was saying what they did was
okay. I used to think forgiving meant I was agreeing to the choice
that person made that caused hurt. But forgiveness does not in
fact mean what someone did was okay. It is saying, "While what
you did hurt me, it will not dictate my life, and I am not going to
project what you did on the other relationships in my life."

I had a list of people I didn't want to forgive or stop myself from
being angry at. I had every right to be angry. There was betrayal
and gossip. There was abandonment, and there were lies. They
went on to live their lives with no consequence I could see to the
huge stain their words had left on my life. They were the same
friends who contributed to my loneliness. I had hosted parties for
them, hosted women's Bible studies with them, and celebrated their
engagements in my backyard. During my divorce, their husbands
chose a side and those same women followed suit. Though I never
wanted them to choose a side, I bet you can guess—they didn't
choose mine. I don't really know if I blamed them . . . I definitely
would not have wanted to create a division in their households,

but it was something that really hurt. And maybe I can understand because I had done that, too, in my past. Being on the other side of anything sure does convict us and give us a taste of the reality of our choices . . . of our judgments. I now know what the pain of quiet betrayal from friends feels like. Not only did I need to forgive this group of individuals, I also needed to forgive myself and seek forgiveness for treating others that way in the past.

This is the messy part of community. If the people who make up community are truly present in their story, they aren't scared of yours. If they aren't present in their story, it can often lead to a lot of hurt toward yours.

So, why did I need to forgive? That was a hard question for me to answer, and I actively talked to God about it. But what I knew was that the Greek word for *forgive* means to release or pardon. I love that definition . . . *release*. The reason I needed to forgive from a practical standpoint was that, while I did not have a relationship with some of these people, they were occupying my headspace. I needed to release how much space they were taking up. That is prime real estate that I needed to fill with something that was actually life-giving and not life-taking. Over lunch one day, when I was sharing with my friend Marla about this chapter, she told me her grandma always used to say, "Unforgiveness does more damage to the place in which it is stored than to the person in which it is poured."

From a spiritual sense, I am no judge, nor should I seek vengeance for anyone's wrongdoing. I have learned that God is my Protector, because when I have given him injustices, he's handled them far better than I would have. Jesus died on the cross not just for my sins but also for the sins of anyone who has hurt me, and by choosing to be angry and hold tight to unforgiveness, I am not receiving the selfless love and act that Jesus chose. Forgiving that group is saying not only do I release you from my headspace but I also believe you are worthy of love, and I believe Christ did not die for only me to live freely.

Who do you need to release who holds space in your mind? I am aware that this small section of the book will not cover all the

UNFORGIVENESS
DOES MORE ⁑
DAMAGE
TO THE PLACE
IN WHICH IT IS
STORED THAN
TO THE PERSON
IN WHICH
IT IS POURED.

complexities of forgiveness. I know some circumstances make it so painful to approach the idea of forgiveness. If *forgiveness* means to release, what amazing possibilities would lie ahead if you were to release from your mind those who have caused you pain, freeing up the space they occupy?

I believe healing is connected to forgiveness. The space in your mind where someone is residing can one day heal, but it takes forgiveness. I think sometimes we need the permission to be angry before we can hold out our hands, allow God to take the anger from us, and ask him to teach us how to forgive what feels unjust.

Forgiveness is active. It does not sleep. It is to be extended to all our relationships. And, oh, how I pray that we desire for it to be living inside our communities. Forgiveness may be working in the headspace of our friends after we've made choices we need to be forgiven for. It also may be looking inside ourselves and identifying what is in the way that's hindering our movement forward. What is taking up space?

Have you heard the phrase "Hurt people hurt people"? It's absolutely true. We do that. Hurt people hurt people because they are scared to get hurt again. And the truth is, we are all degrees away from each other's hurt. Communities are filled with hurting people, but what helps us survive and thrive is our presence in our story. Our choosing to seek forgiveness so we may heal a wound. Choosing to see what Christ did on the cross for us and knowing that Christ did that for our offender too.

I know I will encounter different seasons of life that require courage and extreme acts of forgiveness. There will be circumstances that will make this incredibly difficult and, honestly, really hard to accept. It is okay if you are not there yet, but let your acknowledgment be an opportunity to pray that the Lord will help you with this, because we just can't do it alone, and God wouldn't want us to.

When I asked my dad about forgiveness, he said, "Sometimes I think God allowed me to have my business for forty-five years for many reasons, and one of them would be to learn forgiveness.

Leading a business with hundreds of employees taught me that the flaws of humanity are to be forgiven. I can't think of anybody who has worked for me that I haven't been able to forgive. There does come a time when it becomes our ethos, and it is somewhat natural for us to forgive; we feel it so strongly! I don't know if I have been tested to the max, but I have been tested. Over the years, I've continued to practice understanding my spirituality in Christ so I can let go of anger and hold on to forgiveness just as Jesus demonstrated for us."

As I learned how to better extend forgiveness, I stopped saying that what I was feeling was "bad" or "wrong." Because honestly, it was understandable for me to be angry, but—to take advice from my dad—I didn't need to stay there. And if I stayed there in unforgiveness land, I would eventually spew unforgiveness out on people who didn't deserve it. I had to accept the invitation to forgive people regardless of whether anybody ever apologized. I needed to address it. I wanted to live out of the freedom and forgiveness I could choose rather than living out of the wounds others inflicted.

So if forgiveness is linked to healing, who do you need to forgive? If it is true that to love others, we must love ourselves, I think it is safe to say that to forgive others, we must learn to forgive ourselves.

What do you need to forgive yourself for so you can also extend forgiveness to others? How can you forgive those in your life who have hurt you? Who do you need to ask forgiveness from?

Friend

friend | \ˈfrend\
one attached to another by respect

It was winter and I decided to start running. Winter in Georgia feels like spring in many other states.

I do what most women think they're supposed to do when they decide to start exercising. Go buy a Lululemon matching set and new shoes. I was proud of myself for just wanting to go for a run, and I thought if I looked just right, I'd be more likely to commit to this discipline, so I treated myself to a new running outfit.

I began gradually building up some strong stamina. I started with a mile, then three, and got up to about six miles a day. One day, I started late and ended up running into the evening. As the sun began to slowly go down, I was still about three miles from home. I lived in a high-crime area and wasn't super comfortable running at night. But I had my favorite running outfit on, so I threw on some good music and decided to book it home, thinking, *Eryn, you got this.*

As I ran home, I turned down a street with a cobblestone sidewalk, and continued on my way until I came to an immediate stop. And by *stop*, I mean I tripped and screamed profanities as I flew through the air as if I were Superman. I landed hard and skidded across the cobblestone. It took everything my little body had to stop myself from rolling into the middle of the road.

Thanks to my screams, the entire neighborhood was privileged to discover what Superman would look like if he were 4'11" and decked out in Lululemon. The four cars of people who watched it unfold each rolled down their windows to ask if I was okay. Because my adrenaline was at an all-time high, it was hard to tell if my knees were bleeding profusely or if they just stung from landing on cobblestone. Out of embarrassment, I snapped up quickly and told the people in the passing cars I was okay but, dang, that hurt.

I wobbled on for a minute, but then the pain and embarrassment hit me, and I collapsed on the ground and started crying. Maybe I was a little dramatic, but sometimes you just need a good cry. I finally picked myself up and wobbled home in the dark. My knees were so banged up I didn't take my running outfits out of their drawer for a month.

Sometimes, when we're scared, we start running so hard and so fast, we lose sight of the path beneath our feet. In those times, we need friends who are willing to stop us before we take a big fall. But sometimes we don't listen, or it's too late and we crash . . . hard. In those times, we need friends who will pick us up and ask if we're okay.

The truth is, some friends don't stop for us when our life goes crashing forward. Some friends just keep driving, scared to look out the window at the mess we are either currently creating or sitting on the ground with. Friends who passively drive by, maybe even side-eye looking through the window, do not deserve to sit in your story. They need to keep driving. They do not need to know the details. They do not get that honor. It would be an honor for them to hear the worst parts of you because it would take *immense* strength for you to vocalize them.

While it is really painful when the people you thought would stop, get out, and even give you a ride home do not do that, let that be an awareness of where they are in their life. It is not as much of a reflection of you as it is of them.

Sometimes they shouldn't stop, and that is okay because they're not fully capable of sitting with you in your story. But those who lean out of your journey to healing leave room for those who will lean in.

Hardship is one of the best, though certainly not the easiest, ways to find out who your true friends are. The ones who are loyal and understanding, who put you above their egos—let's talk about those friends.

A good friend is

honest
accepting
understanding
loyal
consistent
respectful
trustworthy

In order to have good friends, you have to desire to be a good friend. And before you can be a good friend and love others, you have to be able to love yourself. You know the bumper stickers that say "Love God, Love People"? I think they should actually say "Love God, Love You, Love People."

A good friend doesn't harshly judge during a hard season; they cling to their values and lean in when the hard season comes. We lean on our friends' faith when we don't have it, and we lean on our friends' values and confidence when ours have dissipated. A good friend isn't a yes-man to your choices; a good friend is a yes-man to who you are and who you can become. You don't get where you want to go in life by being around people who make you feel good about whatever choice you make.

During the low times in my life, I looked around at people I admired, and I started to study their lives. And do you know what the common thread was in their community and friendships? They were about values, not interests. It wasn't about how cool they dressed, the trendy things they were associated with, which hobbies they dabbled in, or how they decorated their homes but instead, it was about what they wanted to be known for and how they served each other—the legacy they hoped to leave and where they got their hope from.

Interests come and go, but values remain. Interests do bring people together—sometimes people you'd never imagine being in the same room with—and that can be beautiful. But if I had to choose between the two, I'm prioritizing values every time. When I started praying over my dreams and desires, God started bringing people into my life who had the same values. I felt less lonely, less crazy, less pressure. With friendships based on values, there is a beautiful dynamic that takes shape . . . you learn from each other and grow together. Ironically, you may never find a shared interest. I have friends from different backgrounds, religions, and cultures. We have different interests, but we maintain beautiful friendships because we value the same things: respect, honesty, trustworthiness, loyalty, and consistency.

Sometimes in friendships, we have to read between the lines. There was a time when I had just moved into a new apartment, unsure of how I was going to afford toilet paper, let alone groceries. I survived on the eggs, peanut butter sandwich, and Eggo diet. After work, my friend Amy called and asked if I wanted to get dressed up and go somewhere for some wine and tapas. I immediately said yes because I was so desperate to get out of the house and eat something different. She said she'd come over, we could eat dinner, and then go. I never want to be Debbie Downer and limit the fun, but I said, "How about I meet you. I'm almost done making waffles [aka making Eggos in the toaster]." Amy replied, "Waffles?! Nope. I'm coming over," and she showed up a few minutes later with my favorite meal from a nearby sushi restaurant.

Amy thought she was just being sweet and cute, but she didn't know the impact of that gesture. I was living with a scarcity mindset, trying to get my bearings and rebuild my relationship with money. Amy's kindness meant the world to me. She showed me that she understood. She read between the lines—lines I didn't even draw—and knew what I needed. She knew because she had been in that space before and knew how much debt controls our actions. Amy demonstrated that she saw me and cared for me, just as another friend did for her when she was in my shoes. Which made me so excited to be able to pay it forward to my friends.

It's our ability to read between the lines not drawn that helps us develop deeper connections and stronger friendships. But we have to have the desire to do so. It would have been easy for Amy to keep her head down and say, "Okay, see you after dinner then." Sure, I would have been fine with my Eggos, and we would have had a nice night. But it wouldn't have had a profound impact on our friendship, and I wouldn't be writing about it in this book.

Instead, Amy's gesture said to me,

You're not alone.

I'm here for you.

This is temporary.

You've got people who care, and I'm one of them.

Being around loyal, understanding friends helped me pivot my life as I continued to grow and believe in my worth. And it helped me choose what to value and what kind of friend I want to become.

Letting someone know you care and reminding them that their circumstances are temporary can be one of the biggest gifts and provide a weary soul the hope it needs.

The duet of a friendship is

Love and loss.

Happiness and sadness.

It's pain. It's joy. It's forgiveness.

It's learning to ask for help.

It's learning to give help.

It's learning to walk toward the things that make us human.

Walking toward the hard things about us along with the fun things about us.

It's vulnerability and risk and stepping out of isolation.

How have friends read between the lines and shown up for you in ways that you didn't know you needed? How have you read between the lines to show up for the people you love? What are some friendships you can choose to intentionally invest in to deepen the connection and create a safe space to vulnerably experience the joys and pains of life?

Honesty

hon·es·ty | \ˈä-nə-stē\
fairness and straightforwardness, character, goodness, and integrity

You know those flags at the beach that tell you how safe the water is? The purple one means dangerous marine life, like sharks or stingrays. The red one means high hazard . . . strong currents, high surf. The yellow one means medium hazard . . . moderate surf and currents. Lastly, the green one, the flag we all hope for, designates calm conditions. It basically means, "Go for it."

What about in life? Have you ever found yourself navigating the flags? Or helping a friend navigate them? I know I've pushed forward in the face of situations that would have warranted red or purple flags . . . dangerous, high hazard situations. Despite recognizing the danger, I have still waded out into hazardous waters. I've also been the lifeguard for my friends, throwing every color flag I could find at them, only to watch them swim in dangerous conditions anyway.

While there have been plenty of times I've wished I hadn't ignored the flags, the consequences of ignoring them have helped me understand myself, be more honest about my circumstances, and pay better attention in the future.

When you're stuck in a tidal wave, you don't know whether you're swimming toward the bottom of the ocean or toward the shore, moving sideways or going up for air; all you can do is try to keep your head above water. It's so important in that time to have one or two people—it doesn't need to be, like, twenty—who can be part of throwing the raft. Maybe they go underwater to find you, but the goal is to bring you up for air and help you to safety.

So, how do you know who those people are? Who's trustworthy? Truthfully, in the midst of the tidal wave, you may not know who to trust because maybe you still don't trust yourself. You don't even trust where you're at. You thought you could trust yourself this whole time, but you got yourself into the dangerous waters, caught up in the unpredictable tide. So, who do you trust?

I love what Psalm 116:6 says, that God protects the simplehearted —and *simplehearted* can mean straightforward, honest. The person with a humble heart recognizes their circumstances, can accept that they need help, and is honest with the confusion. God protects us. He protects the simplehearted. And what is even more beautiful—in the space of learning to be honest and seeking whom to trust, the friends who are honest about their past and about their current state won't be scared of your honesty.

Friends who are honest are a gift.

Not only does God desire to guard and protect you but he will use specific people to speak into your life and be a part of the tidal wave.

For me, it's been the friends in my life with whom I've been super honest, straightforward, and vulnerable to the point where I sometimes flinch because I think, *Uhhh, they're not gonna love me anymore*—and yet, the honesty of my struggle does not threaten them; they love me more because I had the bravery to be honest. Those friends know what it's like to have compassion and grace extended to them when other people judged them, and they know how compassion and grace brought them to a place of healing and safety instead of judgment.

FRIENDS WHO ARE [HONEST] WON'T BE SCARED OF YOUR HONESTY.

So I want to encourage you . . .

At the beginning of a hard season . . .

Be honest with your circumstances.

Know that God promises to guard and protect you.

Find humility and acceptance that this wave is beyond your control.

Surrender to his plan. His timing will look different than yours.

Remain open to the people he brings into your life.

And pray for peace and the discernment for the next steps.

It's friendships of honesty and faith that we can lean on when we feel hopeless, unprotected, confused, and faithless.

Are there things you're afraid to share with the people in your life? How can you be more honest in those relationships? On the flip side, can you extend compassion to the people who honestly share their circumstances with you? Ask God for discernment as you cultivate more honesty in your life.

Lighthouse

light·house | \\'līt-,haủs\\
a structure containing a beacon light to warn or guide
ships at sea in darkness

It was spring, which in Georgia feels like summer. I was sitting outside a coffee shop, waiting to meet with a friend. I was experiencing a lot of confusion and pain and was hoping to share these struggles with her.

She grabbed her coffee and met me outside. We made small talk for a minute before I finally blurted out, with zero restraint, some of the choices I had made during my separation. I wanted so badly to get it off my chest that I just word-vomited, believing she was a person I could trust with my story. I thought she was . . . she seemed like she was . . . she'd felt she could trust me with her story, so why wouldn't it be reciprocated? She was by far my closest friend at the time.

But in one moment, the conversation and our friendship completely pivoted. I'll never forget the way she looked at me with complete disgust and judgment. That was the last time for a while that I shared the stirrings of my heart or confided in someone about the decisions I was making.

I don't share this story to garner sympathy or to bring shame to how she responded to my confession . . . but simply to say the response we receive when we share what we're going through, especially from someone we love and care about, shapes our willingness to be vulnerable with them or someone else again.

Secrets manifest when kept in the dark. Whatever we don't bring to light only grows in the dark. What we keep in secret, we keep in isolation. And isolation leads us to rationalize and make choices outside our character. If we struggle with vulnerability, chances are high that in the past someone used our vulnerability against us. In fact, maybe they judged us. If we don't know who we are and whose we are, then knowing who to trust is hard.

I've had a few other conversations resembling the one I described with my friend, and afterward, I told myself I couldn't be honest about my struggles with anyone. I believed it would scare them off. Judgment can bring shame if we allow someone else's opinion to be the solution to our unanswered questions, to define who we are. So, instead of risking being judged, I avoided intimacy altogether. But as I leaned more and more into seeing myself through the lens of God and not the lens of others, I began to see judgment as an opinion and not an answer. I became more willing to step out of isolation and take the risk of being vulnerable.

I attended an all-girl school when I was young, and I grew up with all sisters, which naturally molded my view of sisterhood. But let's be honest, ladies, female friendships are tough, and lasting ones are hard to find. I've been the girl who judges, and I've been the girlfriend who supports. And when I judged, it really had nothing to do with who my friends were or what they did; my reactions stemmed from how high or low my confidence meter was at the time.

I have, in the heat of the moment, decided I was appointed to make a decision about someone else's life before I was ever given the authority to do so. But through being on the other side of judgment, I realized I have a responsibility to become a safe person for people who desire to be seen. Not only have friendships changed my outlook on life but they have also given me a newfound thick skin to endure a friend's shame story and respond in a way that will bring them closer to safety and not further into isolation. The discovery of your true value deepens your capacity to do that. And what an honor it is to sit across from someone baring their heart and respond out of love just as God has done for us.

I have prayed for women who were many steps ahead of me to be the big sister/mentor/friend I needed in my life. Women who were resilient, but not hardened. Women who were a force, but soft. Women who were a safe place to help me process life. If you are a guy, I know that friendships can look different for you. There is a mask that's pretty easy to put on, and deep talk sometimes isn't the natural default. But you can pray for men who want to better themselves. Men who desire to be a better leader and will wrestle with the difficulty of defining what that means.

Did you know that before lighthouses were physical structures, they were just big bonfires in the sand? Now lighthouses are positioned in the most treacherous parts of land in order to bring ships home safely. Lighthouses are navigational guides. They have homes in rugged terrain, where they shine light for all to see. They do not choose the ships they save. Lighthouses are willing to be in the most unsafe spaces to bring home those being tossed along the shore.

My God is that too. He has been my rock in the most treacherous waters. He's navigated me back home when I was far off. God doesn't choose the people he is close to. He is close to all who are weary, and I would say we are all weary in one area of our life or another. God sees us in our darkest moments, and instead of turning off his light, he shines it directly on us to bring us home to safety when we are terrified and confused. When we don't know where we are sailing to. When we think we know the path in the rocky waters, we learn we are in fact farther from the shore.

And as God has done that for me, so have my friends when I did not see God's light flashing at me. He brought people who would

LIGHTHOUSES ARE WILLING TO (BE) IN THE MOST UNSAFE SPACES ← → TO BRING HOME THOSE BEING TOSSED ALONG THE SHORE.

be willing to come into the rugged parts of my life as a representation of his light. Thank you, Lord, that you use people to bring us to shore. Thank you for showing me the ones qualified to do so.

In darkness, I learned who was willing to be a light for me. People who can sit with us in the darkness are a reflection of God's willingness to sit with us. I have grown from my friends' pursuit of me, and their love toward me in some of the most unlovable times of my life has shown me how to be a friend. It's shown me how I could love. How I could pay it forward confidently. How I could be a lighthouse in the darkness of someone else's life.

If you're torn between isolation and the risk of vulnerability in friendship, worried that someone will look at you with disgust and judgment if you share the stirrings of your heart or the decisions you're wrestling with, then repeat after me:

My worth is not found in them.

My worth is not found in what they say.

My worth is not found in what they don't say.

My worth is found in God, who is in me.

Who are the friends who have been a lighthouse in your life, those willing to walk alongside you in the rugged parts of life and represent God's love? In what moments has God guided you to safety when you've felt terrified or alone? In what friendships can you be a lighthouse?

LOOK OUT

Conclusion

I don't normally read conclusions, either, and my editor isn't making me write this, but I think it is important to share.

The conclusion is—well, there really isn't anything to conclude. Because to conclude is to end, and the discovery of our value is continual. It is asking and searching for understanding.

If you have gotten to the end of this book and still have so many unanswered questions, that's good. Because I don't have all the answers, and I know very well my journey to discovering my value was only the tip of the iceberg regarding this topic.

But here is what I know about the questions you still have . . .

Questions are invitations to vulnerability.

When you ask a question, you are admitting you don't know something and are open to an answer you may not want to hear or one you may be longing to hear. When we admit to having questions, we are exposing what we do not know. And when we can do that, it will eventually lead to growth.

Not having the answer is a form of letting go and an invitation to let God show up.

I want to encourage you to journal specific questions you have. I may have written something you don't agree with, or you may still feel confused about a specific topic. Let that be an opportunity to ask God to reveal an answer to your question.

We choose when we are open with God, and we choose when we decide to be closed off to him. The open-heart surgery that's needed takes place once you start slowly surrendering your will to his and asking him questions. You will start to see the difference between the Holy Spirit and your flesh. To have an open heart means your heart is laid open for repair of defects or damage. My heart has been so damaged, by my doing and by other people's doing, as you've read. God has so much work to do on my heart, and I am still scared to give it to him sometimes. Sometimes out of pride, selfishness, or pure laziness. There are days I don't want to be vulnerable with what feels like an unpredictable relationship I have with him. There have been times I have felt he has affirmed things only to have them end, and I'm left confused. I have questions about why things that seem so unjust happen, why a business transaction fell through, why a spouse made a choice that led to the implosion of a marriage, why a friend can't get pregnant, why good things happen to bad people, why bad people are left roaming around. I'm sure you have many questions too. But questions are okay. They are intimacy builders. Until we meet God face-to-face, though I will more likely be on my knees, all of our questions won't be resolved because the world is too complex to have answers to everything. We don't need to have all our questions answered to live knowing the truth that God is real and so is his love. To know that we are not defined by our pasts, and to know that we are inherently worthy of love, no matter what.

Maybe you've felt weary as you've looked in, looked up, and looked out. There's something I want you to know: the fog will lift, and you will laugh again.

In the middle of your pain, where you felt every single shattered part of your heart slowly break off, you may have questioned whether you would ever be whole again. You may have wondered, even if you glued every piece back together, whether you would be seen as defective.

Well, I once heard someone say, "With awareness from your past, the future pain won't be the same. With awareness, you'll discover how to embrace the cracks and flaws. They will become your place of strength. Because it is within those cracks that someone mutually and beautifully broken now has a place to grab hold of."

I believe this means that God has designed us to love. To love ourselves and to love those around us. I hope to be so comfortable in my cracks and flaws and see them the way God sees them. Accepting God's love for me and living out his love that is in me can literally change the trajectory of someone's life. My hope for you is that, as you understand your true value, you'll embark on a continual discovery of who you are, and whose you are, first. You don't have to change what's happened or what's true about you—your past mistakes, relationship status, or career choice. None of that can keep you from love.

There will be pain, but, oh, there is love. For God is love. And *that* love is the remedy for pain. That love has all the answers to your questions. That love is just the beginning.

NO MATTER MY HISTORY,
PAST MISTAKES,
RELATIONSHIP STATUS,
OR CAREER CHOICE,
I AM WORTHY OF LOVE.
I AM NOT DEFINED
BY MY PAST. I AM
PREPARED BECAUSE
OF IT. WHILE MY OWN
VOICE AND OTHERS
MAY TELL ME DIFFERENT,
I WILL LEAN INTO
THE SAFE PEOPLE
WHO AFFIRM THIS WAY
OF THINKING.

WHEN I ENCOURAGE
OTHERS TO LOVE
THEMSELVES, I AM
ENCOURAGING THEM
TO TREAT THEMSELVES
WITH KINDNESS,
PATIENCE, RESPECT,
AND ALL THAT
EMBODIES LOVE.
WE LIVE OUR LIFE
KNOWING WE
HAVE WORTH.
SO WORTH LOVING.
IT'S A LIFESTYLE.

Afterword

If you have made it this far in the book, you are probably about to make one of the most important decisions of your life. For some of you, you are thinking about starting again or picking up where you left off to continue the journey you started some time ago. You know what you need to do to begin again. While others feel what you just read was the confirmation and boost needed to remain focused on a commitment you recently made. You are now empowered to continue forward.

But there is another group I would like to speak to. This group is standing before a mountain. You are looking at how steep, how wide, how rugged, and how challenging it will be to climb this mountain of change. You are looking up to your past mistakes, current hurts, and recent losses, and you are asking yourself and God, *How will I overcome this?* But let me remind you that you are here for a reason. You are here to show others that the mountain before you can be conquered through God's limitless power and might.

As you take the first step to climb your mountain of self-worth, you will be tempted to opt out, or you will wish you were already transformed or at the finish line. You will be tempted to perform or wear a mask and not put in the work needed to be whole from the inside out. You will be tempted to continue covering up the pain, the hurt, and the lies you have gotten used to telling yourself.

You must resist staying where you are and resist this urge to remain comfortable. This mountain was given to you to reflect God's glory and show other people that it is possible to embrace a life full of hope, joy, and love.

You will be tempted to stay around the base of this mountain and attempt to tell yourself you do not have what it takes to go the distance. But you must remember that the journey of transformation doesn't happen in a day; it happens daily. God does his best work day after day of a relentless pursuit of him. This change will happen each time you get up and remind yourself that you are so worth loving.

Being so worth loving is not something you achieve when you reach the top of the mountain. It is something you possess right now. You are loved right now. There is nothing you can do to escape or run from this truth. God's love is not conditional; it is unconditional.

You are so worth loving even at the base of this mountain and will be equally worthy as you start this climb. When you realize this important truth, it will empower you along the way to keep putting one foot in front of the other. This love will push you to rise above anything and everything that has tried to stop you from reaching your God-given potential.

Will it be hard? Yes. Will you be let down? Yes. Will you want to give up as you attempt to make the climb of your life? Absolutely. But those answers are *not* enough to stop you. You now possess a truth that has set you free forever—God's grace is enough, no matter where you find yourself.

On this climb, you will gain new perspectives, wisdom, courage, and resilience. Every time an excuse tries to creep in, you *will* remember that all things are possible with God. You will remember that God is the One ordering your steps. You must believe that every step on this journey will be beautiful, no matter what comes your way.

We often feel that something must be perfect, spotless, without error, and lacking nothing for it to be beautiful. But that couldn't be further from the truth. The dents, the cracks, the imperfections—those are what make up the imperfectly perfect human life that God created worthy.

So to you, my friend, I ask you to please hold on and keep walking, even when you get tired. Please don't lose hope or quit. Please leave room to be gentle and kind to yourself, even when it feels like the world or this climb may not be.

You are a light in this world.

You are here for a reason.

You have a life filled with purpose.

You are worthy and loved.

You are intelligent and belong.

You are made in the image of God, a holy and divine being.

You are one of a kind.

These are the truths of who you are. And before you know it, you are here at the top of your mountain, declaring the marvelous works of what God has done for you.

Terence Lester,
author and founder,
Love Beyond Walls

Acknowledgments

Where do I even begin . . .

So Worth Loving is a refuge. And it was a refuge for me. These three words came as a whisper but wildly and drastically changed my life. The honest, accepting, inspiring, grace-giving, vulnerable community that makes up So Worth Loving gave me the bravery to be honest with myself, and when I was, that same community helped me navigate a path I had never been on before. There was no shame but acceptance, and that acceptance brought me out of darkness. As we say at So Worth Loving, darkness never stays; the sun still rises.

There are individuals who smiled at me, gifted me lunch, or sent a card in the mail that planted little seeds of hope. There were individuals who would send me direct messages and emails that were the exact words I needed to read.

Thank you to the So Worth Loving community. Thank you to the staff members and interns who believed enough in a dream to sacrifice late nights, offer talents, and provide skills that contributed to our store growth.

Thank you, Mary Chau. You held my hand so many times when I doubted if I could continue being an entrepreneur. You encouraged me to keep going. Thank you, Mary, for loving our customers so well and providing exceptional support to them.

Before a book was thought of, there were people in my life who reminded me I was so worth loving. Thank you to all my friends who would check in on me knowing that the mornings were hard and the nights were harder. To my friends who inspired me with their honesty, acceptance, and understanding.

To my sisters. Jenna, thank you for being an example of what a true wordsmith is. The English-major-meets-poetic-heart in you influenced me growing up and taught me to be brave with words inside my journals.

Tara and my brother-in-law Michael, thank you for being an example of what showing up for family looks like. You graciously give and serve those you love so, so well. I am thankful I got to be a recipient of your generosity.

To Jay. You taught me loyalty and presence. The Lord never leaves us, and he shows up ready to fight our battles, and you were a physical representation of that.

Thank you to one of my best gal pals, Toni Collier. When I didn't know how to ask for help, you read between the lines. You influenced my life with your loyalty and your resiliency in your own story. You taught me how God positions us in each other's lives for a reason, and we are to love, no matter the inconvenience, and make it a party.

And when the book became a real dream to pursue, there were specific people who advised me on a path. Thank you to my mentors Alicia Britt Chole and Elisa Morgan, who have influenced my life as women in ministry and women who have been bold but soft in conquering trials and roadblocks along your journey. You consistently speak into my life and transform my view of who God is by sharing your personal stories with me.

Thank you, Terence Lester and Mike Foster, who took time to read my manuscript and create words for the book that not only touched my heart but will impact the readers of this book. Your words were so carefully crafted, and I know they came from your own healed and redeemed wounds.

Thank you to Jackson, who spoke into the structure and stories. You made sure it was more applicable and simply better.

Thank you to my agent, Alex, my editors, Rachel and Kristin, and all my new best friends at Baker Books. You embraced all my ideas and dreams without hesitation and were ready to make this book the best that it could become. Your belief in me is such a gift.

I know I forgot someone, and by the time this is turned in, I will have kicked myself and you probably will have received a letter or call from me. Just know . . . thank you. Thank you.

I've seen firsthand when a group of people believe in someone and gift that person a patient listening ear. It is the very thing that brought me to writing this book, and my hope is to give others what my friends and family gave me. Belief.

Eryn Eddy is a social entrepreneur, a writer, a speaker, and a creative director. The founder of the lifestyle clothing brand So Worth Loving, Eryn and her work have been featured on CNN and MSNBC and in *Mashable*, *The Oprah Magazine*, *Jezebel*, *Southern Living*, and *Atlanta Magazine*. A frequent guest on podcasts and speaker at conferences and at corporate headquarters, Eryn speaks and writes about personal struggles, community, empathy, entrepreneurship, the power of honest conversations, and the impact of self-doubt. She lives just outside of Atlanta, Georgia.

connect with
eryn

 @eryneddy   @iameryneddy

---

eryneddy.com

live your life
knowing your worth

No matter your past mistakes, your relationship status, your career choice, or the background you came from, you are so worth loving.

Discover more at **soworthloving.com**

Slow down.
Be in the moment.
Be known. Be heard.

Hosts Elisa Morgan and Eryn Eddy are joined by a variety of guests to share personal stories of hope and encouragement. This podcast is for women who are in the trenches of the beautiful and messy moments of relationships, work, ministry, and more.

Listen at **GodHearsHer.org**